SOME OF the earliest references to witchcraft are to be found in the Bible, and magic, witchcraft and sorcery have for centuries formed part of the European experience. In the renaissance of the late fifteenth century a mass persecution of witches began, leaving a trail of fire and blood throughout Germany, England, France and elsewhere. Tens of thousands of innocent men and women fell martyr to popular fear, ignorance and religious dogma, until the great persecutions declined after the notorious Salem witch trials in the New World, more than two hundred years later.

Using carefully edited extracts from trials, pamphlets, tracts, broadsheets, memoirs, statutes, religious treatises and other sources, Roger Hart examines the nature of witchcraft superstition at that time, the early legislation, the identification of witches with traitors and conspirators against monarchy, and local superstition which seemed to demand witches as an object of community fears and hates. He studies the folklore surrounding witchcraft, for example black and white magic, *maleficia* and *beneficia*, pacts with the devil, familiars, black sabbaths, covens, and discusses waxen images and the other means by which witches were alleged to work. He also assesses the place of informers such as Matthew Hopkins, the English witchfinder-general, in helping to inflame Western society during those disreputable years.

Witchcraft

Roger Hart

*"Of wrathful witches this same pamphlet tells,
How most of all on simple folk they work.
What wonders too they may achieve by spells,
God weed them out in every cell they lurk;
God weeds them out, but Satan still doth hatch
Fresh imps, whereby of all sorts he may catch."*

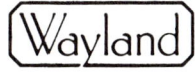

In this series
BATTLE OF THE SPANISH ARMADA   *Roger Hart*
THE BLACK DEATH AND PEASANTS' REVOLT   *Leonard Cowie*
THE BRITISH RAJ   *Denis Judd*
THE HOME FRONT   *Marion Yass*
MEDIEVAL PILGRIMS   *Alan Kendall*
ORIGINS OF WORLD WAR ONE   *R. Parkinson*
ORIGINS OF WORLD WAR TWO   *R. Parkinson*
PLAGUE AND FIRE   *Leonard Cowie*
THE REFORMATION OF THE SIXTEENTH CENTURY   *Leonard Cowie*
THE THIRD REICH   *Michael Berwick*
THE VIKINGS   *Michael Gibson*
WITCHCRAFT   *Roger Hunt*

Cover: A Witches' Sabbath

First published in 1971 by
Wayland (Publishers) Ltd
61 Western Road, Hove
East Sussex BN3 1JD, England

© Copyright 1971 Wayland (Publishers) Ltd

2nd impression 1987

ISBN 1 85210 285 3

Printed and bound at
The Bath Press, Avon, England

Contents

1	How the Great Witch Hunt Began	11
2	Witches or Hags?	25
3	The Satan Worshippers	31
4	The Devil and all his Tricks	47
5	The European Witch Trials	63
6	The English and Scottish Witch Trials	87
7	The Salem Witch Trials	109
	Epilogue	120
	Glossary	121
	Further Reading	123
	Notes on Sources	124
	Index	127
	Picture Credits	128

The Illustrations

Witches flying to a sabbat	frontispiece
A sorcerer conjuring up magic	10
The devil in the shape of a winged goat	13
A witch accepts a "familiar" from the Black Man (Satan)	14
The devil in the shape of a goat	15
Six witchcraft scenes	17
Engraving showing devil's banquet	18
Woodcut showing strange omens in the sky	19
The title page of *Demonology* (1597)	20
A ploughman bewitched by a goblin	22
The devil carrying off a woman	23
A witches' house from *Witchcraft, Magic and Alchemy* (1597)	27
An old woman trying to beat off the devil	29
A crooked bodkin used for pricking witches	30
"The Witches," a famous etching by Goya	33
Satan and a witch, from the *Nuremberg Chronicle* (1493)	34
North Berwick witches examined before King James of Scotland	35
Breughel the Elder's view of the powers of darkness	38–39
Witches receiving images from the devil to use as charms	40
The devil seducing a woman	42
An impression of a witches' sabbat	44
A fairy ring made by spirits dancing in a circle	46
The English witch Anne Bodenham divining the future	52
Witches using magic to raise a storm	54
Witches making flying ointment	57
The devil's tricks	59
The Bamberg witch trials	64
Witches condemned by the Inquisition	68

A courtroom with a witch trial in progress	71
The Bamberg witch trials: an accused man	72
The Bamberg witch trials: a victim brought before a judge	73
Burning witches at the stake in Germany	76–77
English villagers "ducking" a suspected witch	78
Burning condemned witches in Spain	80
A torture chamber of the Inquisition	80
Instruments of torture used in the Bamberg witch trials	82
Dress of condemned witches	84
Pilliwinks used in witch trials	85
The third Chelmsford witch trials (1598)	93
The title page from the *Kingdom of Darkness* (1688)	95
The title page from *Daemonolatria* (1693)	96
English villagers "swimming" an old woman	100
Three witches, from a seventeenth century woodcut	102
Matthew Hopkins, the English witchfinder-general	104
Title page of a pamphlet about the Chelmsford witch trials	106
The title page of *Wonders of the Invisible World* (1693)	111
Cotton Mather	113
A woman seized by a hysterical fit	116
A house at Salem, Massachusetts	117
The slave Tituba telling tales to the Salem children	118

Note on Usage

For the convenience of the general reader, extracts involving archaic language have been rendered in modern English. Spelling and punctuation have been presented in a more consistent and readable form. Sources for all the extracts are given at the end of the book for benefit of those who wish to consult the originals.

R.W.H.

1 How the Great Witch Hunt Began

THE PEOPLE of medieval Europe shared a deep belief in the supernatural. The Kingdom of Darkness, with its devils and evil spirits, was as real and personal as the Kingdom of Heaven; magic could be as powerful as prayer. The idea of supernatural spirits was universal and ordinary folk everywhere believed in demons, imps, goblins and hob-goblins, poltergeists and other spirits, and in legendary creatures such as vampires, werewolves and unicorns.

In the sixteenth century, when the nations of Europe experienced a renaissance of ancient and classical learning, superstitions were as strong—if not stronger—than in earlier generations. The plays of William Shakespeare (1564–1616), for example, are full of allusions to magic. Puck had magical powers (1):

> Sometimes a horse I'll be, sometimes a hound,
> A hog, a headless bear, sometimes a fire,
> And neigh, and bark, and grunt, and roar and burn
> Like horse, hound, dog, bear, fire, at every turn.

Everyone feared signs and portents of evil: "If a hare cross the way at our going forth, or a mouse gnaw our clothes. If they bleed three drops at nose, the salt falls towards them, a black spot appear in their nails, *etc.* (2)."

A later writer was less superstitious: "I am not superstitious in observing nice vanities, such as the falling of pictures, croaking of ravens, crossing of hares, turning over (of) salts, crowning of hens, and such like simple prodigies (3)."

Belief in vampires was a further example of the common super-

Supernatural beliefs

Vampires

Facing page A sorcerer conjuring up magic with a skull and candles, divining rod and cabalistic signs

stitions of many European people. This description dates from as late as 1733: "Vampires issue forth from their graves in the night, attack people sleeping quietly in their beds, suck out all their blood from their bodies and destroy them. They beset men, women, and children alike, sparing neither age nor sex. Those who are under the fatal malignity of their influence complain of suffocation and total deficiency of spirits, after which they soon expire (4)."

Reginald Scot

The English demonologist Reginald Scot (1538–99) remarked how small children were frightened by tales of "bugs" (bogies) by their mothers or maids: "We start and are afraid when we hear one cry 'Boo!' And they have so frayed [frightened] us with bullbeggars, spirits, witches, urchins, elves, hags, fairies, satyrs, Pans, fauns, Silenes, Kit with the canstick, tritons, centaurs, dwarfs, giants, imps, calcars, conjurors, nymphs, changeling, Incubus, Robin Goodfellow, the spoorn, the mare, the man in the oak, the hellwain, the firedrake, the Puckle, Tom Thumb, Hobgoblin, Tom Tumbler, Boneless, and such other bugs, that we are afraid of our own shadows. Insomuch as some never fear the Devil but in a dark night, and then a polled sheep is a perilous beast, and many times is taken for our father's soul, specially in a churchyard, where a right hardy man heretofore scant durst pass by night but his hair would stand upright (5)."

Priests

Priests warned their parishioners to beware of the evildoing of old witches: "Look about ye, my neighbours. If any of you have a sheep sick of the giddies, or a hog of the mumps, or a horse of the staggers, or a knavish boy of the school, or an idle girl of the wheel, or a young drab of the sullens, and hath not fat enough for her porridge or butter enough for her bread, and she hath a little help of the epilepsy or cramp to teach her to roll her eyes, wry her mouth, gnash her teeth, startle with her body, hold her arms and hands stiff, and then, when an old Mother Nobs hath by chance called her an idle young housewife, or bid the devil scratch her, then no doubt but Mother Nobs is the witch, and the young girl is owl-blasted (6)."

Papal Bull of 1484

On 5th December, 1484, Pope Innocent VIII had issued an historic papal bull. This marked the beginning of serious official action against suspected "witches." The bull was widely printed and circulated, and gave much power to the Inquisitors—men

The devil in the shape of a winged goat appearing before people standing in a magic circle (early seventeenth century)

responsible for punishing heresy. "Desiring with the most profound anxiety ... that all heretical depravity should be driven away from the territories of the faithful, we very gladly proclaim and even restate those particular means and methods whereby our Christian endeavour may be fulfilled; since ... a zeal for and devotion to our Faith may take hold all the more strongly on the hearts of the faithful.

"It has recently come to our attention, not without bitter sorrow, that in some parts of northern Germany ... many persons of both sexes, unmindful of their own salvation and deviating from the Catholic Faith, have abused themselves with devils, *incubi* and *succubi*, and by their incantations, spells, conjurations, and other accursed superstitions and horrid charms, enormities and offences, destroy the offspring of women and the young of cattle, blast and eradicate the fruits of the earth, the grapes of the vine and the fruits of trees. Nay, men and women, beasts of burden, herd beasts, as

A witch (*left*) accepts a "familiar" from the Black Man (Satan) in a country lane

well as animals of other kinds; also vineyards, orchards, meadows, pastures, corn, wheat, and other cereals of the earth.

"Furthermore, these wretches afflict and torment men and women, beasts of burden, herd beasts, as well as cattle of all other kinds, with pain and disease, both internal and external. They hinder men from generating and women from conceiving, whence neither husbands with their wives nor wives with their husbands can perform the sexual act.

"Above and beyond this, they blasphemously renounce that Faith which they received by the Sacrament of Baptism, and at the instigation of the Enemy of the human race they do not shrink from committing and perpetrating the foulest abominations and excesses to the peril of their souls, whereby they offend the Divine Majesty and are a cause of scandal and dangerous example to very many (7)."

Inquisitors

The bull decreed "that the aforesaid inquisitors be empowered to proceed to the correction, imprisonment, and punishment of any persons for the said abominations and enormities, without let or hindrance, in every way as if the provinces, townships, dio-

The devil in the shape of a goat carries a candle and broomstick. His worshippers dance around him

ceses, districts, territories, yea, even the persons and their crimes in this kind were named and specifically designated in our letters (8)."

The inquisitors were men appointed by the Holy Office to root out religious heresies, and to see that heretics were punished. The importance of the 1484 bull was that it made witchcraft a heresy. In 1501, Pope Alexander VI gave further papal support to the witch-hunting inquisitors who travelled about Europe, especially in Italy. For "in the province of Lombardy, men and women have abandoned themselves to divers incantations and devilish superstitions, committing infamous crimes by means of poisons (*veneficia*) and divers other practices to destroy men, beasts, and crops, spreading scandalous errors. [Therefore] for the accomplishment of our pastoral duty, as charged by God, we are resolved to suppress such crimes and to prevent, as far as lies in our power, God helping us, the promotion of these scandals and errors.

"For these reasons we thus command you . . . to seek out diligently, either alone or in the company of such honest colleagues as you will select, men and women (as described above), and

The Bible punish and chastise them according to law (9)."

To contemporary scholars, the Bible seemed to state very clearly that witches should be punished. They cited many passages, for example: "Thou shalt not suffer a witch to live (10)." Another line read: "Regard not them that have familiar spirits, neither seek after wizards, to be defiled by them (11)." Or again, "When they say unto you, Seek unto them that have familiar spirits, and unto wizards, that peep and that mutter, should not a people seek unto their God? (12)" Another passage in the Bible told what should be done with witches: "A man or also a woman that hath a familiar spirit, or that is a wizard, shall surely be put to death. They shall stone them with stones; their blood shall be upon them (13)."

Heresy Long ago, Bernard of Clairvaux (1091–1153) had expressed the medieval fear of religious unorthodoxy. Any means could be used to make people keep to the faith: "Faith must be persuaded to men, and not imposed upon them. Yet it would be better that they were coerced by the sword of that magistrate who beareth not the sword in vain, than that they should be allowed to bring many others into their own error (14)."

Devils During the European renaissance, many books about "demons" were published. Many of them contained lists of the various devils which were supposed to infect the witches. Here is such a list, compiled by the Italian friar and scholar, Francesco-Maria Guazzo:

"The first [devil] is the *fiery*, because these dwell in the upper air and will never descend to the lower regions until the Day of Judgment, and they have no dealings on earth with men.

"The second is the *aerial*, because these dwell in the air around us. They can descend to hell, and, by forming bodies out of the air, can at times be visible to men. Very frequently, with God's permission, they agitate the air and raise storms and tempests, and all this they conspire to do for the destruction of mankind.

"The third is *terrestrial*, and these are certainly cast from Heaven to earth for their sins. Some of them live in woods and forests, and lay snares for hunters; some dwell in the fields and lead night travellers astray; some dwell in hidden places and caverns; while others delight to live in secret among men.

"The fourth is the *aqueous*, for these dwell under the water in

Six witchcraft scenes showing (*top*) flying devils, and witches with a wax image, (*middle*) levitation, and the devil appearing as a goat, and (*bottom*) more levitation, and angelic apparition

Engraving dated 1608, showing a devil's banquet. The bewitched guests are served by imps and goblins

rivers and lakes, and are full of anger, turbulent, unquiet, and deceitful. They raise storms at sea, sink ships in the ocean, and destroy life in the water. When such devils appear, they are more often women than men, for they live in moist places and lead an easier life. But those which live in drier and harder places are usually seen as males.

"The fifth is the *subterranean*, for these live in caves and caverns in the mountains. They are of a very mean disposition, and chiefly molest those who work in pits or mines for treasure, and they are always ready to do harm. They cause earthquakes and winds and fires, and shake the foundations of houses.

"The sixth is the *heliophobic*, because they especially hate and detest the light, and never appear during daytime, nor can they assume a bodily form until night. These devils are completely inscrutable and of a character beyond human comprehension, because they are all dark within, shaken with icy passions, malicious, restless, and perturbed. And when they meet men at night they oppress them violently and, with God's permission, often kill them by some breath or touch . . . This kind of devil has no dealing with

Seventeenth century woodcut, showing strange omens in the sky

witches. Neither can they be kept at bay by charms, for they shun the light, and the voices of men, and every sort of noise (15)."

An English writer William West gave his own description of witches, during the reign of Elizabeth I:

A list of witches

"*Magicians* are those who—by uttering certain superstitious words—dare to attempt things above the course of nature, by bringing forth dead men's ghosts, as they falsely pretend, in showing things either secret or in places far off, and in showing them in any shape or likeness.

"*Soothsaying wizards* divine and foretell things to come, and raise up evil spirits by certain superstitious and conceived forms of words. And unto such words as be demanded of them, do answer by voice, or else set before their eyes in glasses, crystal stones or rings, the pictures or images of things sought for.

"*Divinators:* professors of the art of divination who are puffed up with prophesying spirits. And can show who has stolen things and tell where things lost or stolen be.

"*Jugglers* and flighty curers of diseases, who—to cure all sicknesses and sores of man and beast—use either certain superstitious

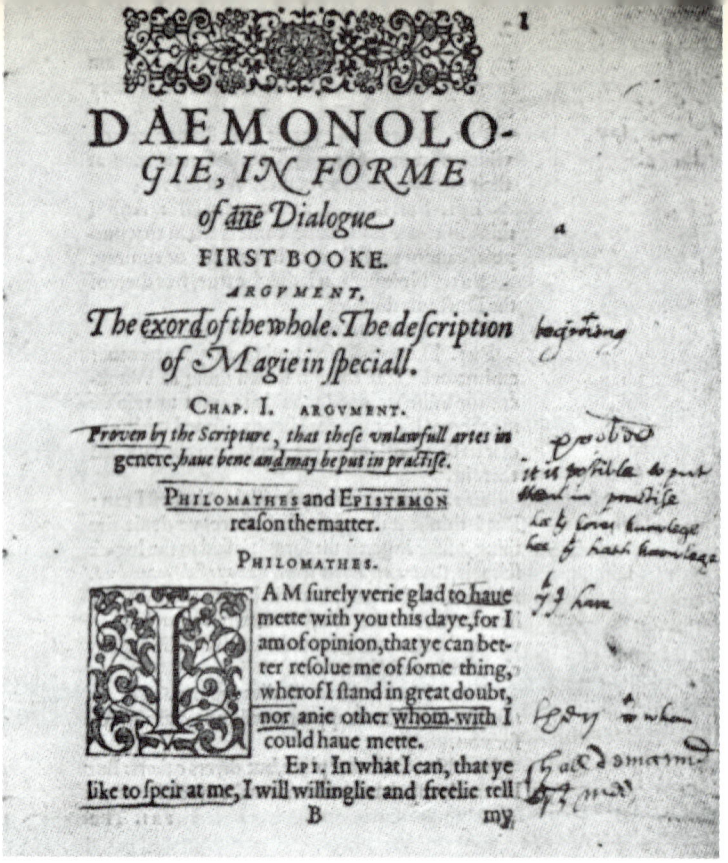

The title page of *Demonology* (1597) written by King James VI of Scotland (James I of England)

words or writings called charms, or spells hanged about the neck or some other part of the body.

"*Enchanters and charmers*, by certain words spoken, and characters or images, herbs or other things applied, think they can do anything they like, the devil so deceives them, or by his action does those things which the enchanters would have done. These are somewhat different from witches or hags, and augurers or soothsayers by birds, diviners by seeing the entrails of beasts sacrificed.

"*Witches*: a witch or hag is she who—deluded by a pact made with the devil through his persuasion, inspiration and juggling—thinks she can bring about all manner of evil things, either by thought or imprecation, such as to shake the air with lightnings and thunder, to cause hail and tempests, to remove green corn or trees to another place, to be carried on her familiar spirit (which has taken upon him the deceitful shape of a goat, swine, or calf, *etc.*) into some mountain far distant, in a wonderfully short space of time, and sometimes to fly upon a staff or fork, or some other instrument, and to spend all the night after with her sweetheart, in playing, sporting, banqueting, dancing, dalliance, and divers other develish lusts and lewd disports, and to show a thousand such monstrous mockeries (16)."

Maleficium

Witches were defined as evil doers: "Witches are those who, because of the magnitude of their crimes, are commonly called *malefici* or evil doers. These witches, by the permission of God, agitate the elements, and disturb the minds of men less trusting in God. Without administering any poison, they kill by the great potency of their charms ... For they summon devils and dare to rouse them so that everyone kills his enemies by evil stratagems. For these witches make use of the blood of victims, and often defile the corpses of the dead ... For the devils are said to love blood, and so when the witches practise the black arts, they mingle blood with water, so that by the colour of blood they can more easily conjure up the devils (17)."

James I

King James VI of Scotland himself wrote a serious book on witchcraft. This was *Demonology*, published in 1597. It took the form of an imaginary debate between two characters. Like most of his contemporaries, James himself never doubted that witches existed: "The fearful abounding at this time in this country of these detestable slaves of the Devil, the Witches or Enchanters, has moved me (beloved reader) to dispatch in post this following treatise of mine ... to resolve the doubting hearts of many, both that such assaults of Satan are most certainly practised, and that the instruments thereof merits most severely to be punished. This is against the damnable opinions of two principally in our age, whereof the one called Scot an Englishman [Reginald Scot] is not ashamed in public print to deny that there can be such a thing as witchcraft: and so maintains the old error of the Sadducees in denying the existence of spirits ...

"And in order to make this treatise more pleasant and convenient, I have put it in form of a dialogue which I have divided into three books: the first speaking of Magic in general, and Necromancy in particular; the second of Sorcery and Witchcraft; and the third a discourse of all these kinds of spirits and spectres that appear and trouble peoples, together with a conclusion of the whole work. My intention in this labour is only to prove two things, as I have already said: the one, that such devilish arts have existed and still exist, the other, what exact trial and severe punishment they merit (18)."

English witch trials

The first witchcraft cases really began in England and Scotland in the 1500s. King James personally intervened in one case of witchcraft in Scotland in June, 1591. A jury had dismissed the charges against one Barbara Napier, much to James's annoyance. Witchcraft, he said, "is a thing grown very common amongst us. I know it to be a most abominable sin, and I have been occupied for three quarters of this year in laws both of God and men that this sin is most odious. And by God's law punishable by death. By man's law it is called *maleficium* or *veneficium*, an ill deed or poisonous deed, and punishable likewise by death.

Wild superstition

"The thing that moved (the jury) to find as they did, was that they only had the testimony of witches, which they thought insufficient. By the civil law I know that such infamous persons are not allowed

A ploughman is bewitched by a goblin at twilight (French)

The devil on a black horse carries off a woman from her home (from a woodcut of 1555)

to be witnesses, except in matters of heresy and *lesae majestatis*. For in other matters, it is thought improper, yet in these matters of witchcraft there are good reasons that such be admitted. First, no honest person can know about these matters himself. Second, because the witches will not accuse themselves. Thirdly, because no act which is done by them can be seen.

"Further, I call those people witches who renounce God and yield themselves wholly to the Devil. But when they have recanted and repented, as these have done, then I account them not as witches and so their testimony is sufficient (19)."

It may seem strange to us that men of scholarship and learning could be so superstitious. When, for example, a ninety-year-old priest cut his throat in 1608, to avoid being burned as a witch, an Italian Friar quickly explained: "A demon appeared to him and tempted him so that . . . he cut his own throat with his knife. And although the wound was not serious enough to cause instant death, yet the demon in that very act of desperation violently seized upon his soul and carried it to hell, to the great astonishment of all. I saw the man dead, and still warm, lying on the straw. And as he had led the life of a beast, so he lay upon the food of beasts. Divine Justice made it so, as it rewards every man according to his works. And God willed that he, who had for ninety years lived a follower of Satan, should also end his life at the hands of Satan (20)."

Thomas Ady

In 1656, the English writer Thomas Ady declared that there was nothing in the Bible to justify witch-hunting: "Where is it written in all the Old and New Testaments that a witch is a murderer, or hath power to kill by witchcraft, or to afflict with any disease or infirmity? Where is it written that witches have imps sucking of their bodies? Where is it written that witches have biggs [nipples] for imps to suck on ... that the devil puts secret marks upon witches ... that witches can damage corn or cattle ... or can fly in the air ... ? (21)."

Thomas Hobbes

The English philosopher Thomas Hobbes (1588–1679) was sceptical about witchcraft, too. But he still thought that the guilty should be punished: "As for witches, I think not that their witchcraft is any real power. Even so, they are justly punished for falsely believing that they can do such mischief, joined with their purpose to do it if they can, their trade being nearer to a new religion than to a craft or science (22)."

Rise of the powers of darkness

But in the late 1500s and early 1600s the sceptics were few. A hundred years had passed since the first papal bull against witches. By this time hundreds of books had been written on the subject, and a great body of superstitious scholarship had grown up. Witchcraft, especially on the European Continent, was counted as heresy, and seemed to threaten the security of religion. It is significant that the great witch hunt roughly coincided with the Renaissance, a period in which the Church everywhere felt itself to be on the defensive against its enemies, both within and without. The devil was seen to be at work everywhere, and the powers of darkness seemed about to envelop the Christian Church. Already, the fear of witchcraft had led to the first executions in Europe. The great witch hunt was getting under way, and Europe was launched on a path of hysteria which would claim at least 100,000 victims—mostly innocent of any crime—until the frenzy died down by the start of the eighteenth century.

2 Witches or Hags?

Old Hags

THE POPULAR IDEA of a witch in towns and country villages was an ugly old hag, twisted by age and spite. Usually, she would keep company with mice or toads, or other "familiar spirits" secretly given to her by the devil. The English poet Edmund Spenser (*c.* 1552–99) pictured a typical witch in her lonely cottage (23):

> There, in a gloomy hollow glen, she found
> A little cottage built of sticks and weeds,
> In homely wise, and walled with sods around,
> In which a witch did dwell in loathly weeds
> And wilful want, all careless of her needs;
> So choosing solitary to abide,
> Far from all neighbours, that her devilish deeds
> And hellish art from people she might hide,
> And hurt far off, unknown, whomever she envied.

Witches were supposed to have an unnatural liking for rats and toads: "Rats and toads are both looked upon as noxious creatures, and therefore generally loathed by all people, who generally have a natural antipathy against that sort of vermin, unless it be witches and such, who are said to cherish them (24)."

Any old woman unlucky enough to be diseased or deformed ran the risk of being branded as a witch. One such in England was Elizabeth Device, a defendant in the much-publicized Lancashire witch trials of 1612: "This odious witch was branded with a preposterous mark in nature, even from her birth: her left eye stood lower than the other, the one looking down, the other looking up, she was so strangely deformed that the best that were present in that honourable assembly and great audience affirmed that they had

Reginald Scot the Sceptic

not often seen anything like it (25)."

Reginald Scot was one of the few writers in the sixteenth century to dismiss witchcraft as mere superstition. He made many enemies. He sympathized with innocent old women who were persecuted as witches. They were "commonly old, lame, bleary-eyed, pale, foul, and full of wrinkles; poor, sullen, superstitious, and papists, or such as know no religion. In their drowsy minds the Devil has taken such a strong hold that whatever mischief, mischance, calamity, or slaughter occurs, they are easily persuaded that it was done by themselves, imprinting in their minds an earnest and constant imagination hereof.

"They are lean and deformed, showing melancholy in their faces to the horror of all who see them. They are doting, scolds, mad, possessed with spirits. They are so firm and steadfast in their opinions, that whoever pays attention to nothing but what they say could easily believe they were true indeed (26)."

An English bishop, writing in 1599, described the witch as a crone: "an old weather-beaten crone, having the chin and her knees meeting for age, walking like a bow, leaning on a staff; hollow eyed, untoothed, furrowed on her face, her limbs trembling with the palsy, going mumbling in the streets; one who has forgotten her Lord's Prayer, but who still has a sharp tongue to call a drab a drab (27)."

It was easy to see how such poor souls could be blamed for other people's misfortunes: "Doubtless at length some of her neighbours die or fall sick, or some of their children catch convulsions, hot fevers, worms, *etc.*, which ignorant parents suppose is the vengeance of witches.

"Yes, and their opinions and fancies are confirmed and maintained by unskilful physicians, according to the common saying *Inscitiae pallium maleficium et incantatio*—'witchcraft and enchantment is the cloak of ignorance.' Whereas in reality evil humours—and not strange words, witches, or spirits—are the causes of such diseases.

"Also, some of their cattle perish, either by disease or mishap. Then those who suffer these misfortunes, consider what people say about this woman (her words, displeasure, and curses so neatly matching their misfortune), and not only imagine—but decide—

A witches' house from *Witchcraft, Magic and Alchemy* (1579) by Gillot de Givry. The witches fly on broomsticks out of the chimney to go to their sabbat

that all their mishaps are brought about by her alone (28)."

Scot added: "These miserable wretches are so hateful to all their neighbours, and so feared, that few dare to offend them or refuse them anything they ask. As a result, they imagine that they can do things quite beyond the ability of human nature.

"They go from house to house and from door to door asking for a pot full of milk, yeast, drink, pottage, or some such relief, without which they could hardly live. And they do not obtain for their service and pains, or by their art, nor yet at the Devil's hands (with whom they are said to make a clear bargain) either beauty, money, promotion, wealth, worship, pleasure, honour, knowledge, learning, or any other benefit at all (29)."

In a seventeenth-century play, *The Witch of Edmonton*, an old

Village gossip

Witch of Edmonton woman complains that she would never have become a witch unless people had forced her into it by their gossip (30):

> *And why on me?—why should the envious world*
> *Throw all their scandalous malice upon me?*
> *'Cause I am poor, deformed and ignorant,*
> *And like a Bow buckled and bent together,*
> *By some more strong in mischiefs than myself?*
> *Must I for that be made a common sink,*
> *For all the filth and rubbish of Men's tongues*
> *To fall and run into? Some call me Witch;*
> *And being ignorant of myself, they go*
> *About to teach me how to be one: urging*
> *That my bad tongue (by their usage made so)*
> *Forspeaks their Cattle, doth bewitch their Corn,*
> *Themselves, their Servant, and their Babes at nurse.*
> *This they enforce upon me: and in part*
> *Make me to credit it.*

Devil marks   In rural areas throughout sixteenth-century Europe, many women were suspected of being witches. But how could their witchcraft be proved? Every witch was believed to have a "devil mark" somewhere on his or her body. This was said to show that a contract had been made with the devil, and so was proof of guilt. An Italian demonologist wrote: "The demon imprints on the witches some mark, especially on those whose loyalty he suspects. That mark, however, is not always of the same shape or kind. Sometimes it is like a hare, sometimes like a toad's foot, sometimes a spider, a puppy, a dormouse. It is imprinted on the most secret parts of the body; with men, under the eyelids or perhaps under the armpits, or on the lips or shoulders, the anus, or elsewhere. With women, it is generally on the breasts or private parts. The stamp which makes these marks is the devil's talon (31)."

Jacques Fontaine   A French doctor, Jacques Fontaine, noted in 1611: "Some say that Satan makes these marks on them with a hot iron and a certain unguent which he applies under the skin of witches. Others say that the devil marks the witches with his finger, when he appears in human form or as a spirit. If it were done with a hot iron, there would clearly be a scar on the part marked, but the witches testify that they have never seen a scar over the mark . . . but it is not

In a lonely country lane an old woman tries to beat off the devil in the shape of a cloven-footed cockerel

necessary to prove this, for the devil, who does not lack knowledge of medications and has the best of them, has only to mortify that place. As for the scar, the devil is such a skilful worker that he can place the hot iron on the body without causing any scar (32)."

One way of identifying a witch was by "pricking" his or her body. "This latter method was linked to the theory of devil's marks, those areas on the skin disfigured by some mole or birthmark or scar, supposedly indicating the possessor's branding by Satan. If a suspected witch had no such obvious marks, she might still have invisible marks, discovered only by pricking. All such devil's marks were reputedly morbid. Thus if a long pin were stuck into them, no pain would be felt and no blood would run out (33)."

Before a witch was "pricked" her entire body would sometimes be shaved. There were three reasons for this: the suspect might have tiny amulets or charms concealed on her person; the devil might be hiding in the witch's hair; and any devil marks had to be closely inspected: "This mark is discovered among us by a pricker,

Pricking

whose trade it is, and who learns it just like any other trade. But it is a horrid pretence for they say that if the place does not bleed, or if the person feels nothing, he or she is bound to be a witch ... A villain who used this trade with us, and who was arrested for other villainies in 1666, confessed that all this trade was a mere cheat (34)."

Inherited witchcraft

Guazzo believed that the powers of witchcraft were passed down from one generation to the next: "The infection of witchcraft is often spread through a sort of contagion to children by their sinful parents, when they try to find favour with their devils. For the greed of Satan has always been limitless and insatiable. Thus, when he has once entered a family, he will never give up his foothold except with the greatest struggle. And it is one of many sure and certain signs against those accused of witchcraft, that one of their parents was found guilty of this crime.

"There are daily examples of this inherited taint in children, for the Devil is always busy to increase the number of his followers. And there can be no better way of doing this than by urging and compelling those who are already in his power to corrupt their own children (35)."

Many victims

When the European witch-hunt was in full swing in the early 1600s, it was only too easy to find plenty of victims. When an innocent mole or scar was taken for a "devil mark," no one could feel safe from the superstition—especially if they were feared or unpopular in their own local communities. In the next chapter we will see exactly how these "witches" were supposed to practise their craft. Some, no doubt, experimented with forms of magic, just as alchemists did in their own way; but most witches were victims of the misinformed and highly-coloured imaginations of the inquisitors.

A crooked bodkin used by witch-finders to "prick" witches for devil marks

3 The Satan-Worshippers

IN THE PERIOD roughly from 1550 to 1700, there grew up an enormous literature of witchcraft. No doubt a few people experimented with magic, as they have done throughout the ages. But much of what was believed about covens, black sabbaths, familiar spirits, and pacts with the devil, was new. As the fear of the powers of darkness spread throughout Renaissance Europe—and indeed to the New World—so scholars everywhere began to set down what they heard. Often their books became accepted as authoritative by judges and lawyers in witchcraft trials. The tragedy was that, in an atmosphere of superstition, the fear and ignorance fed upon itself.

Books on witchcraft

The essence of witchcraft, especially on the European continent, and in Protestant Scotland, was the pact with the devil. The witch gained certain magical powers, and perhaps a "familiar spirit," in exchange for renouncing his or her soul. It was the idea of this pact which enabled both Catholic and Protestant religious leaders to pinpoint witchcraft as heresy, and to punish it as such.

The first full account of a pact with the devil dates from 1435, in a very early printed book on witchcraft. The ceremony was thought to be a parody of Christian baptism: "First, on a Sunday, before the holy Water is consecrated, the future disciple and his masters must go into the church, and there in their presence renounce Christ and his faith, baptism, and the Catholic Church. Then he must do homage to the *magisterulus*, that is to the 'little master' (for so they term the devil). Afterwards he drinks from the flask of liquid taken from murdered infants. This done, he forthwith takes himself to conceive and hold within himself an image of our art and the chief rules of this sect (36)."

Pact with the Devil

Isobel Gowdie's confession

In 1662, a Scottish witch, Isobel Gowdie, confessed to making such a pact with the devil: "As I was going between the farmsteads of Drumdewin and the Heads, I met the Devil and there made a covenant with him. And I promised to meet him in the night time in the kirk [church] of Auldearne, which I did. And the first thing I did then on that night was to deny my baptism, and did put one hand on the crown of my head and the other to the sole of my foot. And then I gave all between my two hands to the Devil. He was in the Reader's desk and had a black book in his hand.

"Margaret Brodie of Auldearne held me up to the Devil to be baptized by him, and he marked me on the shoulder, and sucked out my blood and spat it into his hand. And sprinkling it on my head said: 'I baptize thee, Janet, in my own name.' After a time we went away. The next time I met him was in the New Ward of Inshoch, and he copulated with me. He was a large black hairy man, very cold, and I found his semen in me as cold as spring water. Sometimes he wore boots, sometimes shoes, but his feet were forked and cloven. He told me he sometimes appeared as a deer or a roe (37)." (Note that the Devil re-baptized Isobel under a new name: Janet.)

The Italian scholar, Guazzo, believed that the pact was a parody of the Catholic liturgy:

"1. Denial of the Christian Faith: 'I deny the creator of heaven and earth. I deny my baptism. I deny the worship I formerly paid to God. I adhere to the Devil and believe only in thee.' Trampling the cross, which accompanied this oath, had been from very early times an important part of the ritual.

"2. Rebaptism by the Devil with a new name.

"3. Symbolic removal of the baptismal chrism (the consecrated oil mingled with balm).

"4. Denial of godparents and assigning of new sponsors.

"5. Token surrender to the Devil of a piece of clothing.

"6. Swearing allegiance to the Devil while standing within a magic circle on the ground.

"7. Request to the Devil for their name to be written in the Book of Death.

"8. Promise to sacrifice children to the Devil, a step which led to the stories of witches murdering children.

"The Witches," a famous etching by Goya

Satan and a witch, from the *Nuremberg Chronicle* (1493)

"9. Promise to pay annual tribute to the assigned demon. Only black-coloured gifts were valid.

"10. Marking with the Devil's mark in various parts of the body, including the anus in men, and the breasts and genitals in women, so that the area marked became insensitive. The mark might vary in shape—a rabbit's foot, a toad, or a spider.

"11. Vows of service to the Devil: never to adore the sacrament; to smash holy relics; never to use holy water or candles; and to keep silence on their traffic with Satan (38)."

Devil's pact a blasphemy

References to pacts with the devil are to be found in English witch trials, too, although not as often as on the Continent. A defendant in the famous Chelmsford witch trials of 1589, Joan Prentice, confessed that "the Devil appeared before her in the almshouse aforesaid, about ten o'clock in the night, in the shape and proportion of a dunnish coloured ferret, with fiery eyes. And the said examinate being along in her chamber, and sitting on a low stool preparing to go to bed, the ferret stood with his hind legs upon the ground and his forelegs settled upon her lap, and settled

The North Berwick witches are examined before King James VI (woodcut from *Newes from Scotland,* 1591)

his fiery eyes upon her eyes, and spoke these words to her: 'Joan Prentice, give me thy soul!'

"This examinate was greatly amazed and answered, 'In the name of God, what are you?' The ferret answered, 'I am Satan. Fear me not. I come to do you no harm, but to take your soul, which I must and will have before I depart from you.' The said examinate said that he asked her for something which it was not hers to give, saying that her soul belonged to Jesus Christ alone, by whose precious blood it was bought and purchased.

"The said ferret replied, 'Then I must have some of your blood,' which she willingly agreed to, offered him the forefinger of her left hand. The ferret took this into his mouth so that her finger smarted exceedingly. When the said examinate demanded again of the ferret what his name was, it answered 'Bid'. And then the said ferret suddenly vanished from her sight (39)."

In the trial of Anne Bodenham in 1653 there occurs a description of a similar pact between a maid and the devil: "Then the witch took the maid's forefinger of her right hand, and pricked it with a

Joan Prentice

Anne Bodenham

pin, and squeezed out the blood and put it into a pen, and put the pen into the maid's hand, and held her hand to write in a book. And one of the spirits laid his hands or claw upon the witch's, whilst the maid wrote. And when she had finished writing, whilst their hands were together, the witch said *Amen*, and made the maid say *Amen*, and the spirits said *Amen, Amen*. And the Spirit's hand did feel cold to the maid as it touched her hand, when the witch's hand and hers were together writing (40)."

Shakespeare William Shakespeare referred to the pact with the devil in his play, *A Comedy of Errors* (41):

> *Some devils ask but the parings of one's nail,*
> *A rush, a hair, a drop of blood, a pin,*
> *A nut, a cherry-stone;*
> *But she, more covetous, would have a chain.*
> *Master be wise: an' if you give it to her,*
> *The devil will shake her chain an' fright us with it.*

Black Sabbats The new witch was believed to join other witches in a coven or family of witches, and to worship the devil at "sabbats" (black sabbaths). Witches were believed to fly to their sabbats: "Sometimes witches are really transported from place to place by the devil, who in the shape of a goat or some other fantastic animal carries them bodily to the sabbat . . . This is the general opinion of the theologians and jurists of Italy, Spain, and Catholic Germany, while a great many others are of a like opinion (42)."

In her confession of April, 1662, Isobel Gowdie claimed that she and the other witches in her coven could fly through the air on magical straws: "I had a little horse, and would say *Horse and hattock in the Devil's name*. And then we would fly away wherever we wanted to go, just as straws fly upon an highway. We fly like straws when we please. Wild straws and cornstalks serve as horses for us, and we put them between our legs and say *Horse and hattock in the Devil's name*. And if anyone sees these straws in a whirlwind and does not bless himself, we may shoot him dead at our pleasure. Any that are shot by us, their soul will go to Heaven, but their bodies remain with us, and will fly as horses for us, as small as straws (43)."

Witches were supposed to be able to fly by rubbing themselves with a special ointment. This "flying ointment" was described in verse by the Jacobean playwright Thomas Middleton. It was made from the corpse of a child (44):

Flying ointment

> *There take this unbaptized Brat:*
> *Boil it well: preserve the fat,*
> *You know 'tis precious to transfer*
> *Our 'nointed flesh into the air,*
> *On Moonlight nights, or Steeple-tops,*
> *Mountained, and Pine trees, that like pricks, or Stops,*
> *Seem to our height: High Towers, and Roofs of Princes,*
> *Like wrinkles in the Earth. Whole Provinces*
> *Appear to our sight then, even like*
> *A russet-mole upon some Lady's cheek.*

The English playwright Ben Jonson described a flight of witches in a masque presented to Prince Henry, James I's eldest son (45):

> *Dame, Dame, the watch is set:*
> *Quickly come, we all are met.*
> *From the lakes, and from the fens,*
> *From the rocks, and from the dens,*
> *From the woods, and from the caves,*
> *From the church yards, from the graves,*
> *From the dungeon, from the tree,*
> *That they die on, here are we.*
> *Comes she not yet?*
> *Strike another heat.*
>
> *The Owl is abroad, the Bat, and the Toad,*
>   *And so is the Cat-a-Mountain;*
> *The Ant, and the Mole sit both in a hole,*
>   *And Frog peeps out o' the fountain;*
> *The dogs they do bay, and the Timbrells play,*
>   *The Spindle is now a-turning;*
> *The Moone it is red, and the stars are fled,*
>   *But all the Sky is a burning.*

A description of a witches' sabbat appears in the report of the trial in Scotland in 1591 of Doctor Fian, alleged to be the leader of the North Berwick witches. One defendant, Agnes Tompson, described the sabbat and re-enacted part of it before King James VI of Scotland: "She confessed that on the night of All Hallow's Even

North Berwick witches

Overleaf Breughel the Elder's view of witches, goblins, demons, devils, imps and familiars, and all the powers of darkness

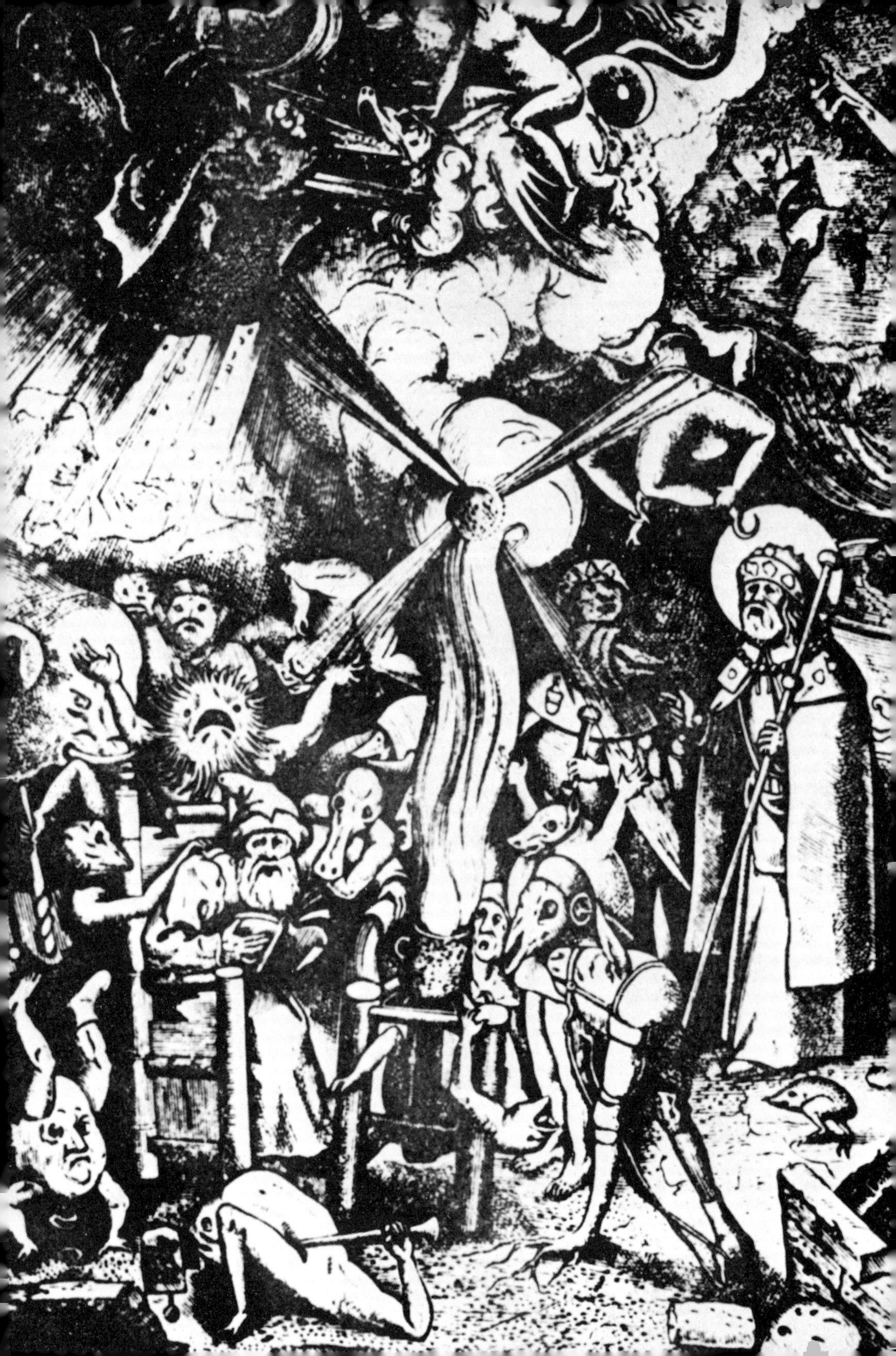

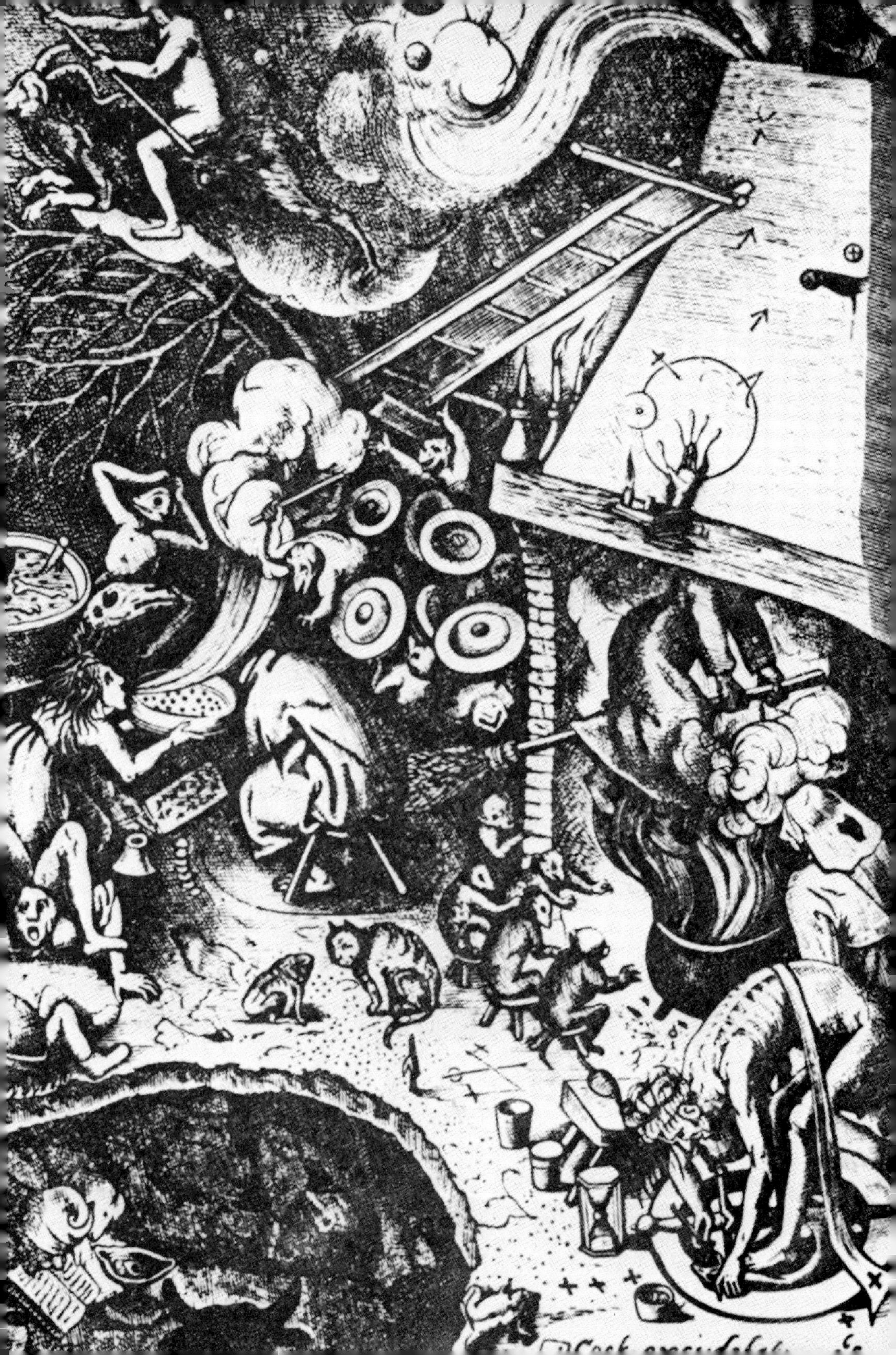

last, she was accompanied both by the persons aforesaid and by a great many other witches to the number of two hundred. And that they all went together by sea, each one in a riddle or sieve, and went in the same very substantially with flagons of wine, making merry and drinking by the way in the same riddles or sieves, to the kirk of North Berwick in Lothian.

"And that after they had landed, they took hands on the land and danced this reel or short dance, singing all with one voice:

> *Commer go ye before, commer go ye;*
> *If ye will not go before, commer let me.*

"At which time she confessed that Gillis Duncan did go before them playing this reel or dance upon a small trump, called a Jew's trump, until they entered the kirk of North Berwick.

"These confessions filled the King with a wonderful admiration. He sent for the said Gillis Duncan, who upon the same trump played the dance before the King's Majesty who, because of the strangeness of these matters, took great delight in being present at their examinations (46)."

Witches receive images from the devil to use as charms

Agnes Tompson then confessed "that the Devil was then at North Berwick kirk awaiting their coming in the guise of a man. Seeing that they tarried over long, he made them all do a penance when they arrived. This was that they should kiss his buttocks as a sign of obedience to him; which being put over the pulpit bar, everyone did as he had told them. And having made his ungodly exhortations, during which he denounced the King of Scotland, he received their oaths for their loyal service towards him, and departed. When this was done, they returned to sea, and so home again (47)." It was significant that the devil "denounced the king"—for witchcraft was thought to threaten earthly kingdoms as well as heavenly ones.

In France, it was widely believed that thousands of witches regularly met at night to worship the devil. One black sabbat in France was described by a local curé in May, 1669, in Basse-Normandie: "This sabbat was just the same as those described in all the books, at all times and in all places. The witches anointed themselves, and a tall man with horns carried them up the chimney. Their activities followed the established pattern: dancing, what they call their 'pleasure,' cutting infants into little pieces, boiling them with snakes over the fire, taking devil's powder to work *maleficia* [evil], signing the pact with the devil their master in their own blood, the huge goat, right down to the black candles.

French Sabbats

"The only thing peculiar to this sabbat at La Haye de Puits was that the devil, for greater protection, frequently put his mark on his vassals. It was also most unusual that more than a hundred priests were identified. For my part, I am convinced of the truth of everything that was said at the trial, and I believe that the devil in the shape of a rat had really spoken to one of the accused, a boy of ten years (48)."

Isobel Gowdie described the meeting of her coven in Scotland, during her trial in 1662. It was thought to be unusual in having thirteen, not twelve, members. "A Grand Meeting would be held about the end of each quarter. There are thirteen in each coven, and each one of us has a spirit to wait on us when we are pleased to summon him. I do not remember the names of all the spirits, but there is one *Swein*, which waits on Margaret Wilson of Auldearne. He is dressed in grass-green, and Margaret Wilson has a nickname

Isobel Gowdie

The devil seducing a woman from a German woodcut of 1489

Pickle nearest the wind.

"The next spirit is called *Rorie*, and he waits on Bessie Wilson of Auldearne. He is dressed in yellow. Her nickname is *Throw the corn yard.*

"The third spirit is called *The Roaring Lion* and he waits on Isobel Nichol of Lochlow. He is dressed in sea-green. Her nickname is *Bessie Rule.*

"The fourth spirit is called *MacHector*, who waits on Jean Martin, daughter of the said Margaret Wilson. He is a young Devil, clothed in grass-green. Jean Martin is the Register [secretary] for women in my coven, and her nickname is *Over the Dyke With It*, because the Devil always takes the Register for women by the hand when we dance the Gillatrypes, and when he would leap

... he and she will say: *Over the dyke with it.*

"The name of the fifth spirit is *Robert the Rule* and he is clothed in dark brown, and he seems to be the commander of the rest of the spirits. He waits upon Margaret Brodie of Auldearne.

"The name of the sixth spirit is called *Thief-of-Hell-Wait-Upon-Herself*, and he also waits on the said Bessie Wilson.

"The name of the seventh spirit is *The Reed River*. He is my own spirit and waits on me. He is dressed in black.

"The eighth spirit is called *Robert the Jack*. He is dressed in brown and seems to be old. He is an awkward half-witted fool. He waits on Bessie Hay, whose nickname is *Able and Stout*.

"The ninth spirit is called *Laing*, and the woman's nickname he waits on is *Bessie Bauld* (Elsbet Nishie).

"The tenth spirit is named *Thomas-a-Fairy*. There will be many other devils waiting upon our Master Devil, but he is bigger and more awful that the rest of the devils and they all reverence him. I know them all one from another when they appear like men (49)."

Devil worship

There were various accounts of how witches were supposed to worship the devil. This one comes from seventeenth century Italy. "When these members of the devil have met together, they generally light a foul and horrid fire. The devil is president of the assembly and sits on a throne, in some terrible shape, as of a goat or a dog. They approach him to adore him, but not always in the same manner. Sometimes they bend their knees as suppliants, and sometimes they stand with their backs turned, and sometimes they kick their legs high up so that their heads are bent back and their chins point to the sky. They turn their backs and, going backwards like crabs, put out their hands behind them, to touch him in supplication. When they speak they turn their faces to the ground, and they do everything in a manner altogether foreign to other men (50)."

Witch banquets

Several contemporaries recorded that great banquets were held at sabbats: "There are tables placed and drawn up, and they sit down and start to eat the food which the demon had provided, or which they themselves have brought. But all who have sat down to such tables confess that the feasts are all foul either in appearance or in smell, so that they would easily nauseate the most hungry stomach.... They say that there is plenty of everything except

An impression of a witches' sabbat, from a French woodcut of 1640

bread and salt (51)." (Bread and salt were staple items in any normal diet.)

An interesting—if untypical—mention of a banquet in an English sabbat occurs in the Lancashire witch trials of 1612. One of the accused, Old Chattox, recalled: "There was victuals, *viz.*, flesh, butter, cheese, bread and drink ... and after their eating, the devil called *Fancy*, and the other spirit calling himself *Tibbe*, carried the leftovers away. And she said that although they ate, they were never the fuller or better for it. And that at their banquet, these spirits gave them light to see what they were doing, although they had no fire or candle light. They were both she-spirits and devils (52)."

When a witches' coven sat down to feast, a black grace might be recited. Isobel Gowdie confessed in 1662 that "we used to go to several houses at night. Last Candlemas we were at Grangehill, where we had good food and drink in good quantities. The Devil sat at the head of the table, with all the coven around him. That night he desired Alexander Elder of Earlseat to say the grace before meat, which he did. It went thus:

A black grace

> *We eat this meat in the Devil's name,*
> *With sorrow and such and great shame;*
> *We shall destroy house and hold;*
> *Both sheep and cattle into the fold.*
> *Little good shall come to the fore*
> *Of all the rest of the little store* (53)."

The English scholar Henry More (1614–87) claimed to have found proof of dancing devils at an English sabbat: "There was found in the place where they danced a round circle, wherein there was the manifest marks of the treading of cloven feet, which were seen from the day after Nicolea had discovered the business till the next winter that the plough cut them out. These things happened in the year 1590 (54)."

These, at least, are some of the different accounts of pacts, covens and sabbats recorded during the great European witch craze. No doubt some of them had some basis of truth, for throughout the ages human beings have experimented with magic. But many of such acts were confessed to by terrified victims of the

A fairy ring made by spirits dancing in a circle with devils, from Nathaniel Crouch, *Kingdom of Darkness* (1688)

Inquisition, who would admit to anything suggested to them by their accusers to try and escape the horrors of the torture chamber, or of imprisonment at least.

4 The Devil and all his Tricks

TO PEOPLE of the sixteenth and seventeenth centuries, the Devil was just as real a person as God. The struggle between the powers of light and darkness was bitter and endless. Witches were the agents of the Devil, and must be ruthlessly hunted down and killed. For if the powers of God were super-human, so were those of Satan and his witches. If God could work miracles, it was not surprising that Satan was able to wield supernatural power as well. In the accounts of the thousands of witch trials of the period 1550 to 1750, one finds witches credited with the most extraordinary powers—to raise storms, bewitch people, destroy crops by magic, cause sickness and death, and to turn themselves into wolves and vampires.

Light and darkness

In the previous chapter we have seen how a witch was supposed to make the covenant with the devil; and we have seen how the coven celebrated its sabbat and worshipped the devil. But what powers did the witches claim to receive in return? Some witches claimed to be able to turn themselves into animals by the devil's power. They used charms like these: "When we go in the shape of a hare, we say thrice over:

Meta-morphosis

> *I shall go into a hare,*
> *With sorrow and sigh and mickle [much] care;*
> *And I shall go in the Devil's name*
> *Ay while I come home again.*

And instantly we start in a hare. And when we would be out of this shape, we will say:

> *Hare, hare, God send thee care.*
> *I am in a hare's likeness just now,*
> *But I shall be in a woman's likeness even now.*

When we would go in the likeness of a cat, we say thrice over:

> I shall go into a cat,
> With sorrow and sigh and a black shot.
> And I shall go in the Devil's name
> Ay while I come home again (55)."

Corpses The use of corpses for sorcery was rarely alleged in English witch trials. One of the few cases of this occurred in the trial of the Malmesbury witches in 1612. Grace Sowerbutts, a girl of fourteen, testified that the defendants dug up a baby's corpse and used it to change themselves into other shapes. Then, "having it there, they did boil some of it in a pot and some of it on coals, both of which the said Jennet and Ellen did eat. And afterwards the said Jennet and Ellen did seethe the bones of the said child in a pot, and with the fat that came out of the said bones, they said they would anoint themselves, so that they might sometimes change themselves into other shapes (56)."

But under cross-examination Grace Sowerbutts broke down, and admitted she had invented the whole episode. This was the horror of many of the witch trials: the rumours and legends were widely circulated and believed, and it was not surprising to hear an old woman accused of witchcraft reciting in court all the superstitious nonsense she had heard outside.

Magic spells More magic spells used for metamorphosis were described by Isobel Gowdie in her trial in Scotland in 1662:

"If we want to change into a crow, we say three times:

> *I shall go into a crow,*
> *With sorrow, and such, and a black thraw!*
> *And I shall go in the Devil's name,*
> *Until I come home again!*

And when we wish to change back we say:

> *Cat, cat (or crow, crow),*
> *God send thee a black shot (or black thraw)*
> *I was a cat (or crow) just now,*
> *But I shall be in a woman's likeness even now.*
> *Cat, cat (or crow, crow)*
> *God send thee a black shot! (or black thraw)*

If we are in the shape of a cat, a crow or a hare, or any other likeness, and we go to any of our neighbours' houses, who are witches and say:

I (or we) conjure thee Go with us (or me)!

And presently they become as we are, either cats, crows, *etc.*, and go with us wherever we wish (57)."

An example of lycanthropy—a terrible form of metamorphosis—is given in a sixteenth-century Baltic tale: "At Christmas, a cripple boy goes around the country summoning the Devil's followers, who are countless, to a general meeting. Whoever stays behind, or goes unwillingly, is beaten by another with an iron whip till the blood flows, and his traces are left in blood.

Lycanthropy

"The human form vanishes, and the whole multitude become werewolves. Many thousands assemble. Foremost goes the leader armed with an iron whip, and the troop follow, firmly convinced in their imagination that they are transformed into wolves. They fall upon herds of cattle and flocks of sheep, but they have no power to slay men. When they come to a river, the leader strikes the water with his scourge, and it divides, leaving a dry path through the midst, by which the pack go. The transformation lasts twelve days. At the end of this time the wolf skin vanishes, and the human form reappears (58)." Tales and legends such as this were not uncommon in sixteenth and seventeenth century Europe, and were often taken to be true.

Witches were believed to dig up corpses and use them for various black magic purposes: "In order to make men die an evil death, witches will exhume corpses, especially those which have been executed and hanged on the gallows. From these dead bodies, along with all the instruments of torture used by the hangman, they obtain materials for their magic, endowing them with a curious power by their incantations (59)."

In her trial in 1662 in Scotland, Isobel Gowdie described how her coven could destroy a man's crops: "Before Candlemas [2nd February] we went east of Kinloss and there we yoked a plough of frogs. The Devil held the plough, and John Young of Mebestown, our officer [secretary] drove the plough. Frogs pulled the plough like oxen. The traces by which they were harnessed to the plough were

Blighting the crop

made of dog grass; the blade in front of the plough-share was made from the horn of a half-castrated ram, and a piece of ram's horn formed the sock. We went twice round in a circle, and everyone in the coven went up and down with the plough, praying to the Devil for the fruit of that land, and praying that thistles and briars might grow up there (60)."

Isobel Gowdie added that her coven could work other magical tricks. They could blacken all the dyes in a vat: "We took a thread of each colour of yarn that was in the said Alexander Cummings's dyehouse and tied three knots in each thread in the Devil's name. We drew the threads widdershins [counter-clockwise] round the vat in the Devil's name; and thereby spoiled the dye, so that it would only dye black, the Devil's colour, in whose name we took away the right colours that were in the vat (61)."

Village fears In many a small isolated village community, local people would go in fear of some old woman whom they believed to be a witch. What they feared was her *maleficium* or evil malice which might be directed against them. One writer defined *maleficium* as "a vicious act directed against the body, through the power of the Devil in a tacit or public pact entered into with the witch, through the control of nature, and with the help of some person satisfying his own malice, done always, rightly even if obscurely, with the judgment of God permitting (62)."

During the Lancashire witch trials of 1612, Mother Demdike described how a witch expressed her *maleficium*. She could kill with waxen images: "The speediest way to take a man's life away by witchcraft is to make a clay model, in the shape of the person whom they mean to kill, and dry it thoroughly. And when you wish them to be ill in any one place more than another, then take a thorn or pin, and prick it in that part of the model you wish to be ill. And when you wish any part of the body to wither away, then take that part of the model and burn it. And so by that means the body shall die (63)."

Clay images An example of causing *maleficium* with clay images occurs, too, in the trial of Isobel Gowdie. The witches "made an image of clay to destroy the Laird of Park's male children. John Taylor brought home the clay in the fold of his plaid. His wife poured water on it in the Devil's name, and made it soft like a hasty-pudding, and made images of the Laird's sons with it.

"It had all the parts and marks of a child, such as a head, eyes, nose, hands, feet, mouth and little lips. It lacked no mark of a child; and its hands were folded down by its sides. It was as big as a large scone or roll, or a flayed sucking-pig.

"We laid its face to the fire until it shrivelled with the heat. And we put a clear fire around it, until it was as red as a coal. After that, we would roast it now and then. Every other day there would be a part of it well roasted. The Laird of Park's healthy children will be made to suffer by it, unless they find it and break it (64)."

When a waxen image had been made, the witches would chant magic spells before casting it into the fire. "The words we said as we made the image for destroying the Laird of Park's children were: *Death spells*

In the Devil's name, we pour this water on the earth
For long dying and ill health;
We put it into the fire, both stick and stour,
It shall be burnt by our will
As any stubble up a hill.

The Devil taught us the words, and when we had learned them, we all fell down upon our bare knees, with our hair over our eyes and our arms raised, gazing upon the Devil, and said the words thrice over, until it was made. And then in the Devil's name we put it into the middle of the fire (65)."

The Italian scholar, Guazzo, explained how one could tell whether someone was suffering from the *maleficium* of a witch. He listed twenty symptoms of bewitchment: *Bewitchment – or illness?*

"1. First, when the bewitched patient's illness is very hard to diagnose, so that the doctors hesitate and are in doubt, and keep changing their minds, and fear to make any positive statement.

"2. If, although remedies have been applied from the outset, the sickness does not lessen, but rather increases and worsens.

"3. If it does not, like natural sicknesses, worsen little by little; but the sick man often suffers the severest pains at the outset, although there is no apparent pathological reason for it.

"4. If the sickness is very erratic; although it may occur periodically, it is seldom regular; and although it may resemble a natural

The English witch Anne Bodenham divining the future, with dancing spirits and a pot of burning coals

disease, it is still different in many ways.

"5. Although the sick man often suffers the greatest pain, yet he cannot say in which part of his body he feels the pain.

"6. From time to time, the sick utter the most mournful sighs, for no apparent reason.

"7. Some lose their appetite, and some disgorge their food and are so upset in the stomach that they are constricted with pain. A kind of lump may be seen rising and falling from the stomach to the throat; and if they try to expel it when it is rising in the throat all their efforts are useless, although it may very soon come out by itself.

"8. They feel pricking pains near the heart, and say that it is being torn in half.

"9. In some the pulse may be seen beating and, so to speak, trembling in their necks.

"10. Others have excruciating spasms in their necks or kidneys or the pit of their stomachs, and often an icy wind passes through their stomach and quickly back again; or they feel a vapour like the fiercest flame attacking them in the same manner.

"11. Some become sexually impotent.

"12. Some are overcome with a sweat, especially in the night, even though the weather and the season are cold.

"13. Others seem to have parts of their bodies twisted up in knots.

"14. The sicknesses of the bewitched are usually a wasting or weakening of the entire body and a loss of strength, with a deep tiredness, dullness of mind, various melancholy ravings, various kinds of fever, which makes a great deal of work for the doctors; certain convulsions like an epileptic; a kind of rigidity of the limbs which looks like convulsions; sometimes the whole head swells; or a great fatigue overcomes the whole body until they can hardly move at all.

"15. Sometimes the whole skin, but usually only the face, turns yellow or ashen.

"16. Some have their eyelids so stuck that they can hardly open them. They can be identified by certain tests.

"17. Bewitched people can hardly bear to look upon a priest, at least not directly, for they move the whites of the eyes in different ways.

"18. When the charms are burned, the sick usually change for the worse, or suffer some harm, according to whether their bewitchment was slight or severe. Often they are forced to utter terrible cries and roars. But if no change or any new lesion can be detected, there is a good chance that the patient will with some attention recover his good health.

"19. If by chance the witch should come near the sick man, the patient is immediately filled with great uneasiness and shakes with fear and trembling. If it is a child, it at once begins to cry. Its eyes turn black, and other strange changes are to be seen in the sick man.

"20. Finally, if the priest seeks to heal the disease by applying holy liniments to the eyes, ears, brow, and other parts, and a sweat or other change appears in those parts, it is clear that the patient is bewitched (66)."

Ointments It can easily be imagined how—in the days when medicine was primitive—various ailments could be mistaken for bewitchment: paralysis, lockjaw, fevers, anaemia, sclerosis, epilepsy, hysteria. Such illnesses often displayed symptoms which were extremely frightening to educated and uneducated people alike.

Witches were sometimes charged with making magical ointment to bewitch someone. Often the ointment was made from the corpses of children. At the Chelmsford trials of 1616 Susan Barker was charged that she "feloniously did take up a skull out of a certain grave in the burial ground of the parish church of Upminster aforesaid, being part of the body of a certain deceased man lately buried there, with intent to use the said skull in certain evil and devilish arts, namely witchcrafts, charms and sorceries, with intent to bewitch and enchant a certain Mary Stevens (67)."

Witches were said to use charms—magic prayers—to strengthen

Witches using magic to raise a storm, from Ulrich Molitor, *De Lamiis* (1489)

the powers of their herbs or amulets. Here is a charm to cure a bewitched person (68):

To cure bewitchment

> *Upon Good Friday, I will fast while I may,*
> *Until I hear them knell*
> *Our Lord's own bell;*
> *Lord in his mass*
> *With his twelve apostles good,*
> *What hath he in his hand?*
> *Liking, lithe wand*
> *What hath he in his other hand?*
> *Heaven's door key.*
> *Open, open, Heaven, door keys.*
> *Steck, steck (shut), hell door.*
> *Let chrisom child*
> *Go to its mother mild.*
> *What is yonder that casts a light so farrandly (splendidly)?*
> *My own dear son that's nailed to the tree.*
> *He is nailed sore by the heart and hand,*
> *And holy harn-pan (skull).*
> *Well is that man.*
> *That Friday spell can,*
> *His child to learn;*
> *A cross of blue, and another of red,*
> *As good Lord was to the rood (cross).*
> *Gabriel laid him down to sleep*
> *Upon the ground of holy weep (i.e. Gethsemane).*
> *Good Lord came walking by:*
> *Sleepest thou, wakest thou, Gabriel?*
> *No, Lord, I am sted (beset) with stick and stake,*
> *That I can neither sleep nor wake.*
> *Rise up, Gabriel, and go with me,*
> *The stick nor the stake shall never deer (harm) thee.*
> *Sweet Jesus, our Lord, Amen."*

Those alleged to practise "white" witchcraft were just as liable to persecution as those who practised black arts. White magic was used for beneficial purposes, rather than to cause harm. One white witch was Alexander Drummond. He was indicted in Edinburgh in 1630 for "curing by witchcraft of frenzies, the falling evil, persons mad, distracted, or possessed with fearful apparitions as

White witches

St Antony's fire, the sickness *noli-me-tangere* [do not touch me], cancers, worms, glengores, with other uncouth diseases upon many persons ... He confesses that such and such cures he did, but denies any incantation or charm therein. For verification of the ditty, produced his own depositions, then the depositions of an hundred of witnesses; whereupon, convicted and burned (69)."

Witches' panacea

A witch in seventeenth-century Scotland described how white magic could be used to cure sickness: "When we wished to heal any sore, or broken limb, we would say three times:

> *He put the blood to the blood, Till all up stood;*
> *The lith to the lith, Till all took with;*
> *Our Lady charmed her darling son,*
> *With her tooth and her tongue*
> *And her ten fingers*
> *In the name of The Father, The Son, and The Holy Ghost.*

And this we say three times, stroking the sore, and it becomes whole (70)."

This white magic spell was used to cure sciatica, or "pains in the haunches:" "We are here three Maidens charming the beanstalks; the man of the Middle-earth, blow beaver, land fever, manners of stores, the Lord frightened the Fiend with his holy candles and yard foot stone. There she sits and here she is gone. Let her never come here again (71)."

And these words could cure all fevers: "I forbid the quaking-fevers, the sea-fevers, the land-fevers, and all the fevers that ever God ordained, out of the head, out of the heart, out of the back, out of the sides, out of the knees, out of the thighs, from the fingertips to the extremities of the toes. Out shall the fevers go, some to the hill, some to the hap, some to stone, some to the stock. In St Peter's name, St Paul's name and all the Saints of Heaven. In the name of the Father, The Son and The Holy Ghost (72)."

The so-called "white witch" used his or her powers for good, to cure sickness or to drive away storms. But the Church disapproved of witchcraft of all kinds: "For if a man's child, friend, or cattle be taken with some sickness or strangely tormented with some rare and unknown disease, the first thing he does is to bethink himself and enquire after some wise man or wise woman, and there he

Opposite Witches seething bones in a cauldron to make flying ointment, a woodcut by Hans Baldung

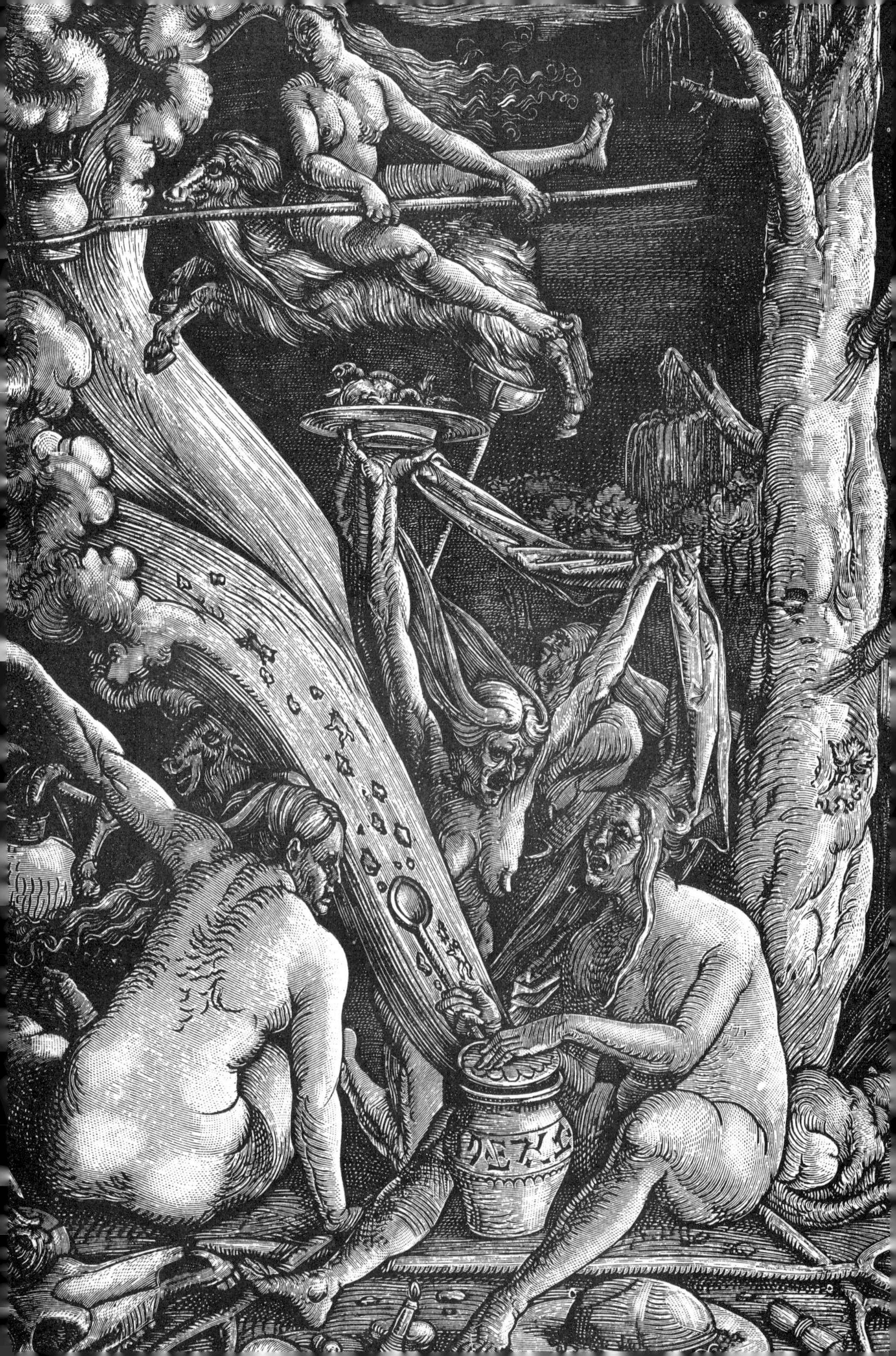

sends and goes for help . . . And the party thus cured cannot say with David, 'The Lord is my helper,' but 'The Devil is my helper!' for by him he is cured (73)."

Storm raising

Witches were credited with all sorts of supernatural powers. For example, they could raise storms: "They tie three knots on a string hanging at a whip. When they loose one of these, they raise tolerable winds. When they loose another, the wind is more vehement. But by loosing the third, they raise real tempests, as in olden times they used to raise thunder and lightning (74)."

Guazzo noted that "witches have confessed that they made hailstorms at the sabbat, or whenever they wished, to blast the fruits of the earth. To this end, according to their confessions, they beat water with a wand, and then they threw into the air or into the water a certain powder which Satan had given them. By this means, a cloud was raised which afterwards turned to hailstones, and fell wherever the witches wished. When water was lacking, they used their urine (75)."

A number of magic spells were described by Isobel Gowdie in her confession of 1662. This was how they raised a wind: "When we raise the wind, we take a piece of cloth and wet it in water, and we take a washerwoman's 'beetle' [flat piece of wood for beating clothes] and beat the cloth on a stone, and we say over it three times:

> *I beat this cloth upon this stone*
> *To raise the wind, in the Devil's name.*
> *It shall not be allayed until I please again.*

When we would lay the wind, we dry the rag and say three times:

> *We lay the wind in the Devil's name,*
> *It shall not rise until we wish to raise it again.*

And if the wind will not lie instantly, we call upon our spirit and say to him: 'Thief! Thief! Conjure the wind and cause it to lie!' We have no power over rain, but we can raise the wind when we please. He made us believe that there was no God but him (76)."

The judges' questions

How did accusers and judges decide whether or not a person was bewitched? A number of scholars published lists of the symptoms of the bewitched. Here is one such list which was consulted in German courtrooms:

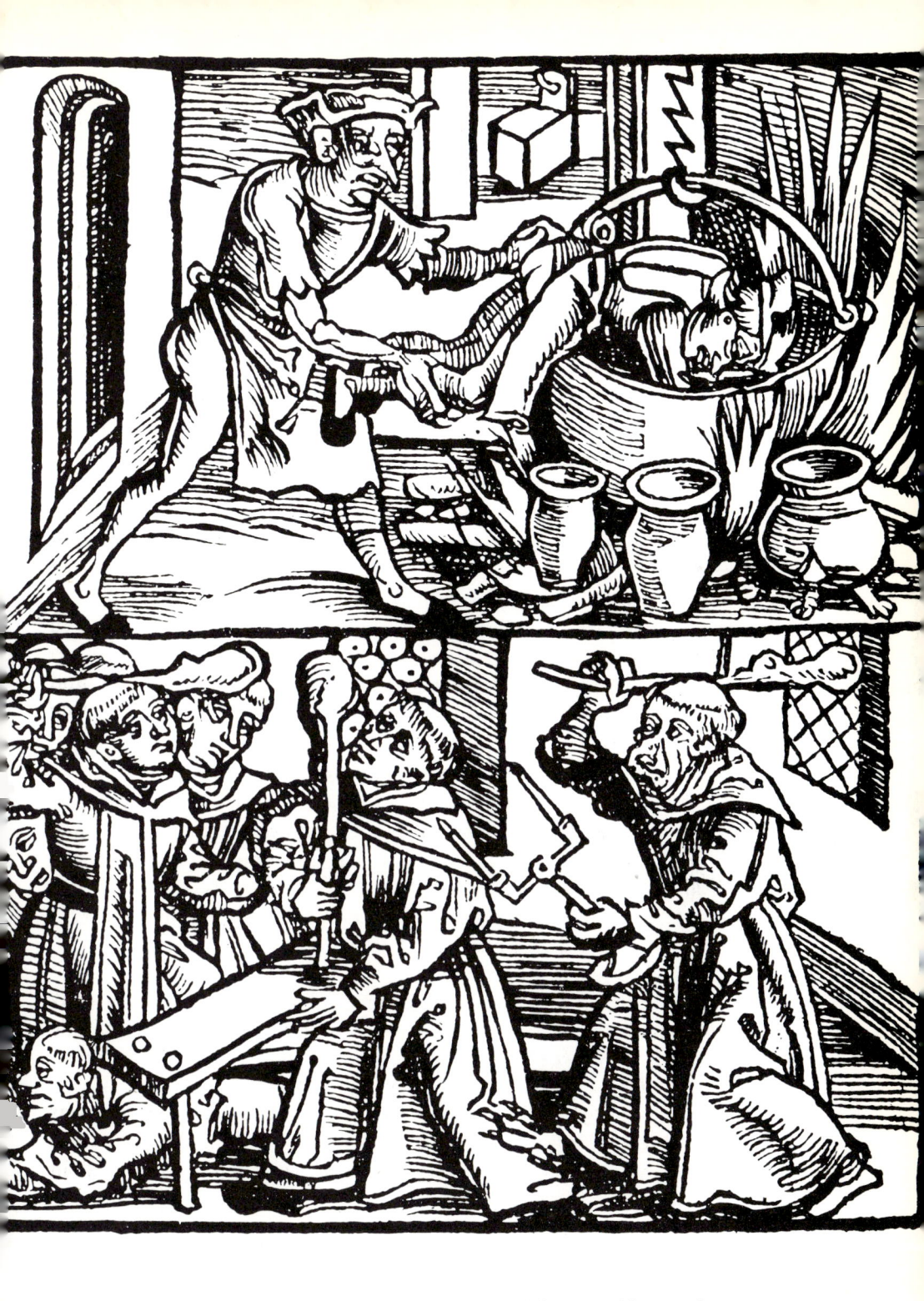

The devil's tricks. *Above* a poltergeist pushing a cook into a cauldron, and *below* the devil disguised as a monk interrupting a mass

"1. The bewitched desire the worst food.

"2. They cannot hold down their food, are irked by continual vomiting, and are unable to digest.

"3. Others experience a heavy weight in the stomach, as if a sort of ball ascended from the stomach into the gullet, which they seem to vomit forth, yet still it returns to its original position.

"4. Some feel a gnawing in the lower belly. Others feel either a rapid pulsation in the neck or pain in the kidneys. Others feel a continuous pain in the head or brain, beyond endurance, which makes them seem oppressed, shattered, or pierced.

"5. The bewitched have trouble with their heart, which feels as if torn by dogs, or eaten by serpents, or pierced by nails and needles, or constricted and stifled.

"6. At other times, all parts of their head swell up, so that throughout their body they feel such lassitude that they can scarcely move.

"7. Some experience frequent and sudden pains, which they cannot describe, but they shriek aloud.

"8. In others, the body is weakened and reduced to a shadow on account of extraordinary emaciation, impotency of vigour, and extreme langour.

"9. At other times, their limbs feel whipped, torn, bound, or constricted, especially the heart and bones.

"10. Some are accustomed to feel something like the coldest wind or a fiery flame run through their stomach, causing the most violent contractions in their entrails and intense and sudden swelling of the stomach.

"11. Many bewitched are oppressed by a melancholy disposition. Some of them are so weakened that they do not wish either to speak or converse with people.

"12. Those injured by witchcraft may have their eyes constricted, and the whole body, especially the face, almost completely suffused by a yellow or ashen colour.

"13. When witchcraft has by chance befallen the sick, he is generally attacked by some serious trouble, seized with fear and terror; if he is a boy, he immediately bewails himself and his eyes change to a dark colour, and other perceptible changes are observed. Wherefore the discreet exorcist takes care to disclose the recognized signs of this sort to the relatives and those present to avoid scandal.

"14. It is especially significant if skilled physicians are not sure what the affliction is, and cannot form an opinion about it; or if the medications prescribed do not help but rather increase the sickness.

"15. Some times the only indications of bewitching are considered circumstantial and inferential, as employing witchcraft for hatred, love, sterility, storm-raising, ligature, or (harm to) animals (77)."

This list of symptoms of the bewitched is very similar to that drawn up by Guazzo (see page 51) in Italy. This shows how much ideas on witchcraft circulated in Europe, and how much they were believed.

Another charm against bewitchment was quoted in the Lancashire witch trials of 1612 (78):

> *Three Biters hast thou bitten,*
> *The Hear, ill Eye, ill Tongue:*
> *Three bitter shall be thy boot,*
> *Father, Son, and Holy Ghost*
> *a God's name.*
> *Five Pater-nosters, five Ave's,*
> *and a Creed,*
> *In worship of five wounds*
> *of our Lord.*

A person could be cured of his bewitchment by this white magic: "If a child is bewitched, we take the cradle . . . throw it three times through an enchanted hoop, ring or belt, and then a dog throws it; and then shakes the belt over the fire . . . and then throws it down on the ground till a dog or a cat goes over it, so that the sickness may leave the sick person and enter the dog or cat (79)."

Attempts might be made to end bewitchment or possession by devils, by means of Christian exorcism: "Fixing his eyes firmly on the possessed person, and laying his hand on his head, in this position, with a secret command to the devil, because the devil himself is the originator of evil, the exorcist makes a certain sign, urging the possessed man publicly:

"I.N., minister of Christ and the Church, in the name of Jesus

Exorcism

Christ, command you, unclean spirit, if you lie hid in the body of this man created by God, or if you vex him in any way, that you at once give me some clear sign of the certainty of your presence in possessing this man . . . which until now in my absence you have been able to do in your usual manner (80)."

Not everyone believed in the power of exorcism. Here is a satirical view (81).

> *Holy water come and bring,*
> *Cat in salt for seasoning,*
> *Set the brush for sprinkling;*
> *Sacred spittle bring ye hither,*
> *Meal and it now mix together,*
> *And a little oil to either.*
> *Give the tapers here their light.*
> *Ring the saints' bell to affright*
> *Far from hence the evil sprite.*

But even today, exorcism remains a recognized Christian method of dealing with the powers of darkness, and priests are sometimes called upon to exorcize—if not a person—then at least a place said to be inhabited by evil spirits.

5 The European Witch Trials

ALTHOUGH THE INQUISITION—the Holy Office to combat heresy—had been founded in 1199, not until the papal bulls of the late fifteenth century, and the publication of *Malleus Maleficarum* (*The Hammer of Witches*) (1486) did the witch hunt really begin. From that time until its decline in the late 1600s and early 1700s, the number of executions for witchcraft reached the appalling total of 100,000. Of these only 5,000 or so took place in the British Isles; most took place in Germany, which was unrivalled in Europe for the barbarity shown to its accused. But France, Italy, Spain, Scandinavia and other parts of Europe, too, have a record of considerable injustice, prejudice and cruelty.

Malleus Maleficarum

The persecution in Germany began about the time of the publication of *The Hammer of Witches*. Soon after, in 1532, the many states which comprised the Holy Roman Empire adopted the Carolina Code which imposed torture and death for witchcraft; and in 1563 the Council of Trent resolved to win back Germany from Protestantism to the Catholic Church. One of the effects of this was to stimulate religious persecutions of all kinds: and witchcraft was a heresy which was zealously hunted down by Protestants and Catholics alike.

Germany

The history of witchcraft in France went back at least to 1398, when the University of Paris had declared that the witches' pact with the devil was not merely superstitious magic, but religious heresy. In 1431, Joan of Arc herself had been accused of the heresy of witchcraft. But the real witch hunt in France did not begin until the early 1500s, much as across the Rhine; and in France, as elsewhere, the delusion was shared by some of her greatest scholars,

France

Wo du Gedult hast in der Pein,
So wird sie dir gar nützlich seyn
Darumb gib dich willig darein.

The Bamberg witch trials. Accompanied by a monk with a cross, a condemned witch is led out of prison to be burned at the stake

for example Jean Bodin, whose book *Demonomanie* (1580) was a landmark in the persecution.

It has often been asked—how, in the European Renaissance, could these terrible delusions have persisted? How could educated scholars, bishops and lawyers have believed in the great witch delusion? The answer is not easy to find. Some historians have shown that the Renaissance revived pagan superstitions and cults whose origins lay in the ancient world. Others again have suggested that, feeling itself menaced by the rebirth of classical learning, the Christian church unleashed an Inquisition as terrible as that of the middle ages, in a supreme effort to destroy the powers of darkness.

The harsh methods of the Inquisition have been summarized as follows:

"1. The accused was presumed guilty until he had proved his innocence. The Inquisition adopted this pivot of Roman Imperial law; but in matters of belief, vindication was almost impossible.

"2. Suspicion, gossip, or denunciation was sufficient indication of guilt to hail a person before the Inquisition.

"3. To justify the activity of the Inquisition, the offence, whatever it might have been, was correlated with heresy. Thus, the men who killed the bigoted Inquisitor Peter Martyr in 1252 were tried, not for murder but for heresy (as opponents of the Inquisition).

"4. Witnesses were not identified. Often their accusations were not made known to the defendant. In 1254 Pope Innocent IV granted accusers anonymity.

"5. Witnesses disallowed in other offences were encouraged to inform against heretics: convicted perjurers, persons without civil rights, children of tender years, and excommunicates (including condemned heretics). If a hostile witness retracted his evidence, he was prosecuted for perjury, but his testimony was allowed to stand. However, according to the Inquisitor Nicholas Eymeric (1360), if the retraction was less favourable to the accused, the judge could accept this second testimony.

"6. No witnesses were allowed to testify on behalf of the accused; nor was his previous good reputation as citizen or Christian taken into account.

"7. The accused was permitted no counsel, since the lawyer would thereby be guilty of defending heresy. (For a short time

WITCHCRAFT IN GERMANY

1486   Publication of *Malleus Maleficarum (Hammer of Witches)* by Jakob Sprenger, Dean of Cologne University, and Prior Heinrich Kramer: a code for witch-hunters

1532   Issue of the Carolina Code. This code imposed torture and death for witchcraft. The code was technically adopted by the 300-odd small independent states which then comprised the Holy Roman Empire

1563   Council of Trent resolves to win back Germany from Protestantism to the Catholic Church: intensification of religious struggles and persecutions

1590   William V begins witch hunt in Bavaria

1618   Start of the Thirty Years War (1618–48) during which the witch hunt throughout Germany was at its height

1628   Trial of Johannes Junius, Burgomaster of Bamberg, for witchcraft

1631   Publication of *Cautio Criminalis* by Friedrich von Spee opposing the witch hunt

1632   Death of the Prince-Bishop of Bamberg marks the end of the terrible persecutions in this large principality (1609–1632)

1655   Last execution for witchcraft in Cologne (where persecution less severe)

1775   Last official execution for witchcraft in Germany (of Anna Maria Schwägel at Kempten in Bavaria)

1787   All witchcraft laws in Austria repealed

lawyers had been allowed, especially when inquisitors were sitting on episcopal courts, and this privilege was resumed in the seventeenth century.

"8. The judges were inquisitors. Occasionally bishops or even laymen were allowed to sit on the *inquisitio*.

"9. The judges were encouraged to trip the accused into confessing. The Inquisitor Sylvester Prierias in 1521 told how this

WITCHCRAFT IN FRANCE

1398	University of Paris declares that the pact with the devil is not merely magic but heresy
1428	Witch trials of Briançon, in the Dauphiné. Some 167 local people burned as witches between 1428 and 1450
1431	Trial of Joan of Arc includes allegations of witchcraft
1440	Notorious trial of Gilles de Rais, accused of witchcraft and debauches
1490	King Charles VIII issues edict against fortunetellers, enchanters and necromancers
1508	Mass witch trials in Béarn
1529	Trial at Luxeuil by the Inquisition
1557	Toulouse witch trials: forty witches burned
1580	Jean Bodin publishes *Démonomanie* condemning witches
1589	Fourteen witches at Tours appeal to King Henry III who is in turn accused of protecting witches
1625	Start of general decline of witch trials in France
1670	Rouen witch trials
1679 to 1682	The notorious *Chambre d'ardenté* affair: Louis XIV's star chamber investigates poison plots, and hears evidence of widespread corruption and witchcraft. More than 300 people arrested, and 36 executed. The affair ended with a royal edict which denied the reality of witchcraft and sorcery.
1745	Last execution for witchcraft in France (of Father Louis Debaraz at Lyons)

could be done.

"10. Although technically allowed only as a last resort, the practice of torture was regularly used, and could be inflicted on any witness. Civil authorities employed torture, but the Inquisition extended and systematized its use. Torture had been sanctioned as a means to discover heresy by Pope Innocent IV in 1257, in a bull *Ad extirpanda*, and was confirmed by later popes; it was not

Witches condemned by the Inquisition were forced to parade in public, carrying candles, and wearing penitential robes and mitres

abolished until 1816 by Pope Pius VII.

"11. Legally, torture could not be repeated, but it could be, and was, legally 'continued' until the accused confessed whatever was demanded of him. Three sessions of torture were usual. Somewhat milder regulations for conducting witchcraft trials were circulated by the Inquisition about 1623.

"12. Having confessed under torture, the accused, in sight of the torture chamber, had to repeat his confession 'freely and spontaneously, without the pressure of force or fear.' Thus he was considered, and the court records so stated, to have admitted his guilt *without torture*.

"13. Every accused had to give or invent names of accomplices or those whom he suspected of heresy.

"14. Generally no appeal was countenanced.

"15. The property of the accused was confiscated by the Inquisition. All popes praised this practice as one of the strongest weapons in the fight against heresy. Innocent IV said it hung like a sword suspended over the heads of heretics and princes. Because confiscation was routine, it was seldom expressly mentioned, save in sentences of excommunication against the dead (82)."

Almost certain death

Once accused in the Inquisition, the victim was launched on a path leading to almost certain death. Before the hour of execution the prisoner was liable to public humiliation: "We enjoin you for your penance the wearing of two crosses of yellow felt, one in front and one behind, on each garment except your shirt. You shall never go about, whether indoors or without, without these crosses being visible. One arm of each shall be twenty inches in length and the other sixteen inches, and each arm of the cross shall be twelve inches in breadth. If they become torn or worn out, you shall repair them (83)."

Cross examination

As the witch hunt developed in Germany, Italy and France, the Inquisitorial courts began to prepare set lists of questions, specially designed to prove a victim's guilt. Here for example are the questions, used by the justices at Colmar in Alsace for some three hundred years (84):

Questions to be asked of a Witch

How long have you been a witch?
Why did you become a witch?
How did you become a witch, and what happened on that occasion?
Whom did you choose to be your incubus?
What was his name?
What was the name of your master among the evil demons?
What was the oath you were forced to swear to him?
How did you make this oath, and what were its conditions?
What finger were you forced to raise?
Where did you consummate your union with your incubus?
What demons and what other humans took part in the sabbat?
What food did you eat there?
How was the sabbat banquet arranged?
Where were you seated at the banquet?

What music was played there, and what dances did you dance?
What did your incubus give you for your intercourse?
What devil's mark did your incubus make on your body?
What injury have you done to such and such a person, and how did you do it?
Why did you inflict this injury?
How can you relieve this injury?
What herbs or what other methods can you use to cure these injuries?
Who are the children on whom you have cast a spell?
And why have you done it?
What animals have you bewitched to sickness or death?
Why did you commit such acts?
Who are your accomplices in evil?
Why does the devil strike you in the night?
What is the ointment with which you rub your broomstick?
How can you fly through the air?
What magic words do you utter then?
What tempests have you raised?
Who helped you to produce them?
What plagues of vermin and caterpillars have you created?
What do you make these pernicious creatures out of and how do you do it?
Has the devil set a limit to the period of your evil-doing?

Bombarded by lists of leading questions such as these, all assuming the victim's guilt from the outset, it is hardly surprising that thousands of innocent people were condemned. Often the victims were poor and ignorant, and easily intimidated by the learned judges who examined them in sombre court rooms. A browbeaten victim might easily misunderstand a question, or fall into some verbal trap. He usually had little chance of avoiding incrimination.

Torture Torture was commonly used to extract confessions: the soul was of more concern than the body. Considering the sophisticated methods of the torture chamber, one need not wonder that torture generally gave the desired results. The German scholar Friedrich von Spee (1591–1635) wrote of forced confessions: "The most robust who have so suffered have told me that no crime can be

A seventeenth century courtroom with a witch trial in progress

imagined that they would not at once confess to, if it would bring even a little relief, and they would welcome ten deaths to escape a repetition (85)."

The French demonologist Jean Bodin (1529–96) justified the use of torture in these words: "If there is any way of appeasing the wrath of God, to gain his blessing, to strike awe into some by the punishment of others, to preserve some from being infected by others, to diminish the number of evil-doers, to secure the life of the well-disposed, and to punish the worst crimes of which the human mind can conceive, it is to punish the witches with the utmost rigour (86)."

Jean Bodin

The *Hammer of Witches* (1486) written by two Dominican friars, suggested detailed rules for the preparatory torture of an unwilling witness: "The method of beginning an examination by torture is as follows. First, the jailers prepare the implements of torture, then they strip the prisoner. If it be a woman, she will already have been stripped by other women, upright and of good report. This stripping is done in case some means of witchcraft may have been sewn into the clothing—such as, taught by the devil, they often

Rules of Torture

The Bamberg witch trials: an accused man is interrogated in a torture chamber equipped with the strappado

prepare from the bodies of unbaptized infants, so that they may forfeit salvation.

"And when the implements of torture have been prepared, the judge, both himself and through other good men, zealous in the Christian faith, tries to persuade the prisoner to confess the truth freely. But, if he will not confess, he bids the attendants prepare the prisoner for the strappado or some other torture. The attendants obey at once, with pretended agitation. Then, at the plea of some of those present, the prisoner is set free again and is taken aside and once more persuaded to confess, being led to believe that if he does he will not be put to death . . .

"But if threats and promises like these cannot induce the witch

The Bamberg witch trials: once accused before a judge, the victim faced almost certain death

to speak the truth, then the jailers must carry out the sentence, and torture the prisoner according to the accepted methods, with whatever severity the delinquent's crime may demand. And, while he is being tortured, he must be questioned on the articles of accusation, and this often and persistently, beginning with the lighter charges—for he will more readily confess the lighter charges than the heavier ones (87)."

Squassation was the last resort of the torturers of the Inquisition: "The prisoner has his hands bound behind his back, and weights tied to his feet, and then he is drawn up high until his head reaches the pulley itself. He is kept hanging in this manner for some time, so that all his joints and limbs may be dreadfully stretched by the

Squassation

weight hanging at his feet.

"Then he is suddenly let down with a jerk, by the slackening of the rope, but kept from coming quite to the ground, by which terrible shake his arms and legs are all disjointed. This puts him to the most exquisite pain—the shock which he receives by the sudden stop of his fall and the weight at his feet stretching his whole body more intensely and cruelly (88)."

Vicious circle

As Friedrich von Spee explained, an accused person who refused to confess was tortured; and then he almost always confessed. No-one could feel safe in their homes. "When under stress of pain the witch has confessed, her plight is indescribable. Not only cannot she escape herself, but she is also forced to accuse others whom she does not know, whose names are frequently put into her mouth by the investigators or suggested by the executioner, or of whom she has heard as suspected or accused. Those in turn are forced to accuse others, and these still others, and so it goes on. Who can help seeing that it must go on and on? . . .

"It is the same with those who are maliciously slandered. If they do not seek redress, their silence is proof of guilt. If they do seek it, the calumny is spread, suspicions are aroused, and it becomes talked about everywhere. Thus, those forced under torture to denounce are likely to name names.

"From all of which follows this, worthy of being noted in red ink: that, if only the trials be steadily continued, nobody is safe, no matter of what sex, fortune, condition, or dignity, if any enemy or detractor wishes to bring a person under suspicion of witchcraft (89)."

No confessions without torture

Von Spee scorned the idea that anyone confessed without torture: "There is a phrase often used by judges, that the accused had confessed without torture and so is undeniably guilty. I wondered at this and made inquiries, and learned that in reality they were tortured, but only in an iron vice with sharp-edged bars over the shins, in which they are pressed like a cake, bringing blood and causing intolerable pain. This is technically called without torture, deceiving those who do not understand the phrases of the inquisitors (90)."

There are several superstitious accounts of people accused of witchcraft who apparently suffered no pain under torture. Guazzo told how "a woman of fifty endured boiling fat poured over her whole body and severe racking of all her limbs without feeling anything. For she was taken from the rack free from any sense of pain, whole and uninjured, except that her great toe, which had been torn off during the torture, was not restored. But this did not hinder or hurt her in any way (91).''

A canon of Treves (a notorious witch-hunting state) declared that witch-hunting had become big business: "This movement was promoted by many in office, who looked for wealth in the ashes of the victims. And so, from court to court through the towns and villages of all the diocese, there scurried special accusers, inquisitors, notaries, jurors, judges, constables, dragging to trial and torture human beings of both sexes and burning them in great numbers.

Witch hunt big business

"Scarcely any of those who were accused escaped punishment. Nor were even the leading men spared in the city of Treves. For the judge, two burgomasters, several councillors and associate judges were burned. Canons of sundry collegiate churches, parish priests, rural deans, were swept away in this ruin. So far, at length, did the madness of the furious populace and of the courts go in this thirst for blood and booty that there was scarcely anybody who was not smirched by some suspicion of this crime.

"Meanwhile notaries, copyists, and innkeepers grew rich. The executioner rode a blooded horse, like a noble of the court, and went dressed in gold and silver. His wife vied with noble dames in the richness of her array. The children of those convicted and punished were sent into exile. Their goods were confiscated. Ploughman and vintner failed—hence came sterility. A direr pestilence or a more ruthless invader could hardly have ravaged the territory of Treves than this inquisition and boundless persecution (92)."

Many people tried to bribe the inquisitors: "It is not unusual that the inquisitor commutes physical into monetary penalties, which has given him a large revenue. Some unfortunate people have to pay a yearly fine. If they stop paying they are once again hauled before the Inquisition. Moreover, as the property of heretics is confiscated by the public treasury, the inquisitor gets a very good percentage of all this.

Bribery

"Finally, a single accusation, a mere suspicion of heresy or

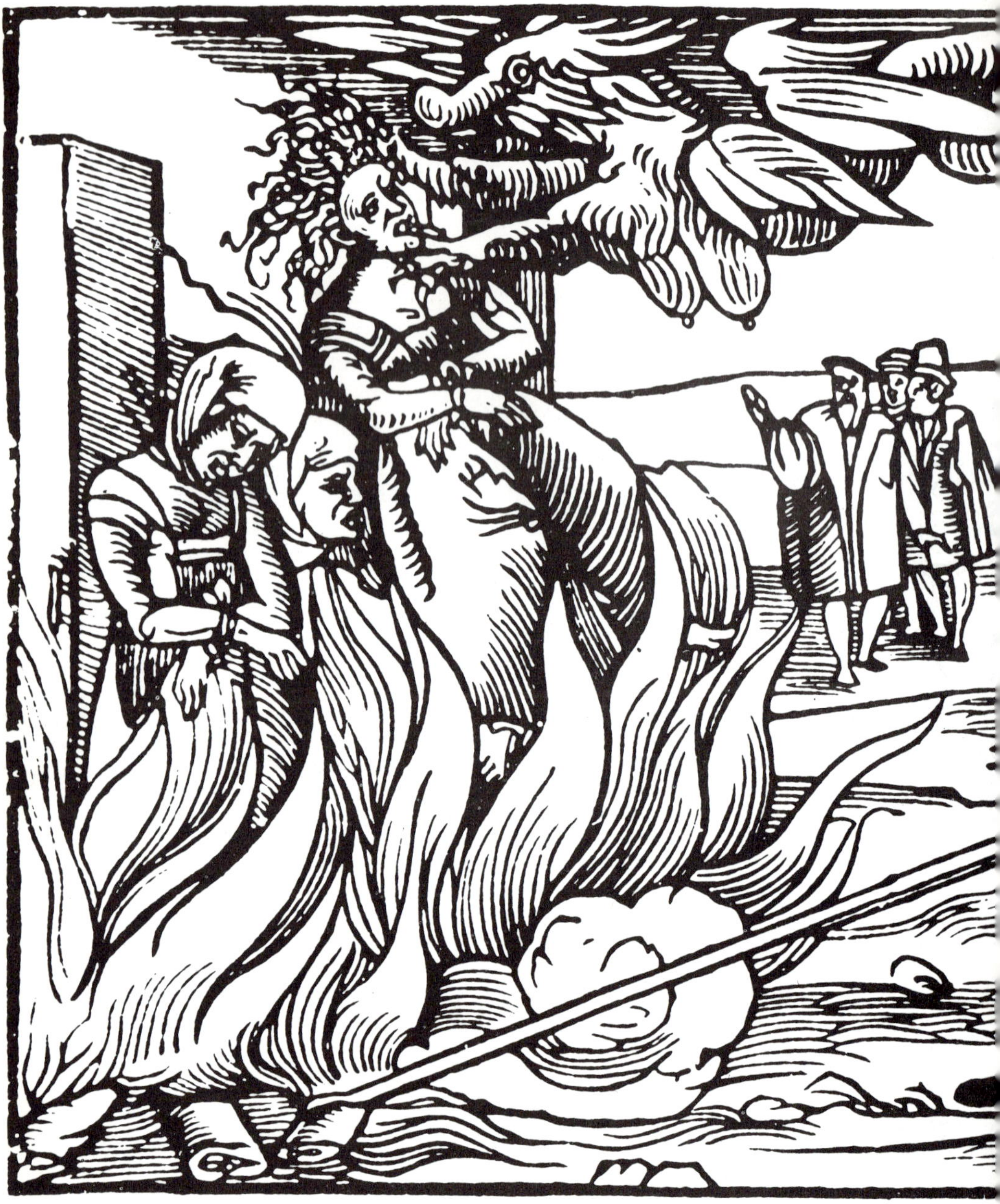

Burning witches at the stake in Germany in 1555. The devil appears as a flying serpent

English villagers of the seventeenth century "ducking" a suspected witch in the river

sorcery, or a citation by the Inquisition, leads to infamy. From this, one is only freed by giving much silver to the inquisitor. While I was in Italy [about 1511–18], most of the inquisitors of the Duchy of Milan were in this way mulcting the most noble ladies as well as poor but honest women, terrorized with fear, from whom they received huge sums of money (93)."

The Bamberg Terror

The persecution in Treves was horrific enough. But of all the three hundred states which made up Germany, the religious principality of Bamberg had the worst record. The witch-hunt was led by the Prince-Bishop Johann von Aschhausen (1609–32) who had some three hundred persons burned as witches, a hundred of them in 1617 alone. In the Bamberg persecutions of the 1620s and 1630s many leading citizens were accused and killed, and Bamberg earned an unenviable reputation for brutality. The tortures included:

"1. The thumbscrews (*Daumenstock*), used in conjunction with
"2. The leg vices (*Beinschraube*);
"3. Scourging either off or while hanging on;
"4. The ladder, a form of strappado;
"5. The stocks (*Bock*), furnished with iron spikes, a torment

which might be continued for as long as six hours;

"6. Strappado (*Zug*), a modification of squassation;

"7. Severe friction with a rope around the neck, to cut to the bone (*Schnur*);

"8. Cold water baths;

"9. Burning feathers (*Schwefelfedern*) held under the arms and groin, frequently dipped in burning sulphur;

"10. Prayer stool (*Betstuhl*), a kneeling board with sharp wooden pegs;

"11. Forcible feeding on herring cooked in salt, and denial of water;

"12. Scalding water baths to which lime had been added (in 1630, six persons had been killed at Zeil by this method) (94)."

One of the saddest records in the history of witchcraft concerns Johannes Junius, the Burgomaster of Bamberg. Junius was accused of being a witch in 1628, tried and burned to death. In the fevered atmosphere of the time, there was nothing he could do. Throughout his trial he protested his innocence. Shortly before he died he scrawled a tragic letter to his daughter Veronica. His writing was almost illegible, because his fingers had been crushed by thumb screws:

Johannes Junius

"Many hundred thousand good-nights, dearly beloved daughter Veronica. Innocent I came into prison, innocent I was tortured, innocent I must die. For whoever comes into the witch prison must become a witch—or be tortured until he invents something out of his head and, God pity him, thinks something up.

Forced confession of Junius

"I will tell you what happened to me. When I was first put to the torture, my brother-in-law, Dr Braun, Dr Kötzendörffer, and two strange doctors were there. Then Dr Braun asked me, 'Kinsman, how come you are here?' I answered, 'Through falsehood and misfortune.' 'Hear, you,' he retorts, 'you are a witch. Will you confess it freely? If not, we'll bring in witnesses and the executioner for you.' I said, 'I am no witch. I have a pure conscience in the matter. If there are a thousand witnesses, I am not worried, but I'll gladly hear them.'

"Then the Chancellor's son was set before me, who said he had seen me. I asked that he be sworn and legally examined, but Dr Braun refused it. Then the Chancellor, Dr George Haan, was

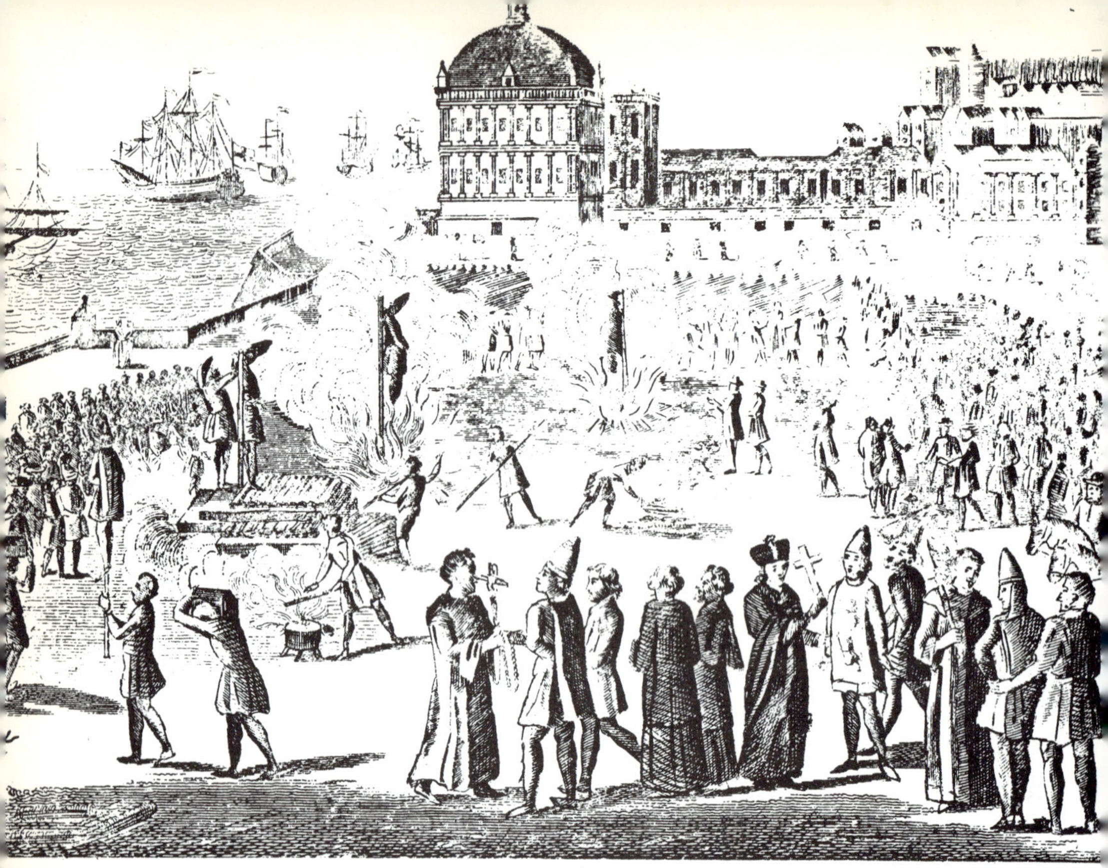

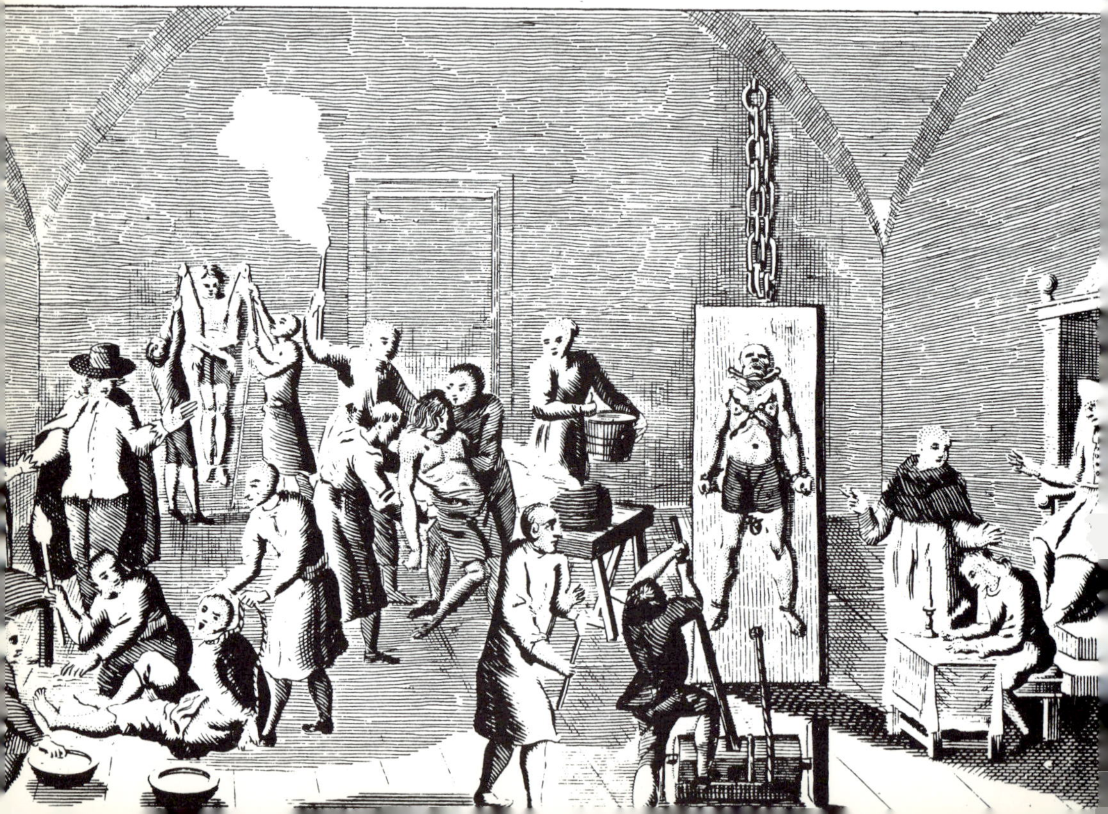

brought, and said the same as his son. Afterwards Höppfen Ellse. She had seen me dance on Hauptsmorwald, but they refused to swear her in. I said: 'I have never renounced God, and will never do it—God graciously keep me from it. I would rather bear whatever I must.'

"And then came also—God in highest heaven have mercy—the executioner, and put the thumb screws on me, both hands bound together, so that the blood spurted from the nails and everywhere, so that for four weeks I would not use my hands, as you can see from my writing.

"Thereafter they stripped me, bound my hands behind me, and drew me up on the ladder. Then I thought heaven and earth were at an end. Eight times did they draw me up and let me fall again, so that I suffered terrible agony. I said to Dr Braun, 'God forgive you for thus misusing an innocent and honourable man.' He replied, 'You are a knave.'

"And this happened on Friday, 30th June, and with God's help I had to bear the torture. When at last the executioner led me back into the cell, he said to me, 'Sir, I beg you for God's sake, confess something, for you cannot endure the torture which you will be put to. And even if you bear it all, you still won't escape, even if you were an earl, but one torture will follow another until you say you are a witch. Not before that', he said, 'will they let you go, as you can see from all their trials, for they are all alike.'

"Then came George Haan, who said that, according to the commissioners, the Prince-Bishop wished to make such an example of me that everybody would be astonished.

"And so I begged, since I was in a wretched state, to be allowed one day for thought and a priest. The priest was refused me, but the time for thought was given. Now, my dearest child, see in what danger I stood and still stand. I must say that I am a witch, although I am not—must now renounce God, although I have never done so before.

"Day and night I was deeply troubled, but at last a new idea came to me. I would not be anxious, but since I had been given no priest with whom I could take counsel, I would think of something myself and say it. It were surely better that I just say it with mouth and words, even though I had not really done it; and afterwards I

Opposite above Burning condemned witches in a public square in Spain.
Below A torture chamber of the Inquisition with the judge seated on the right. The tortures included burning of the feet, strappado, squassation, and burning oil

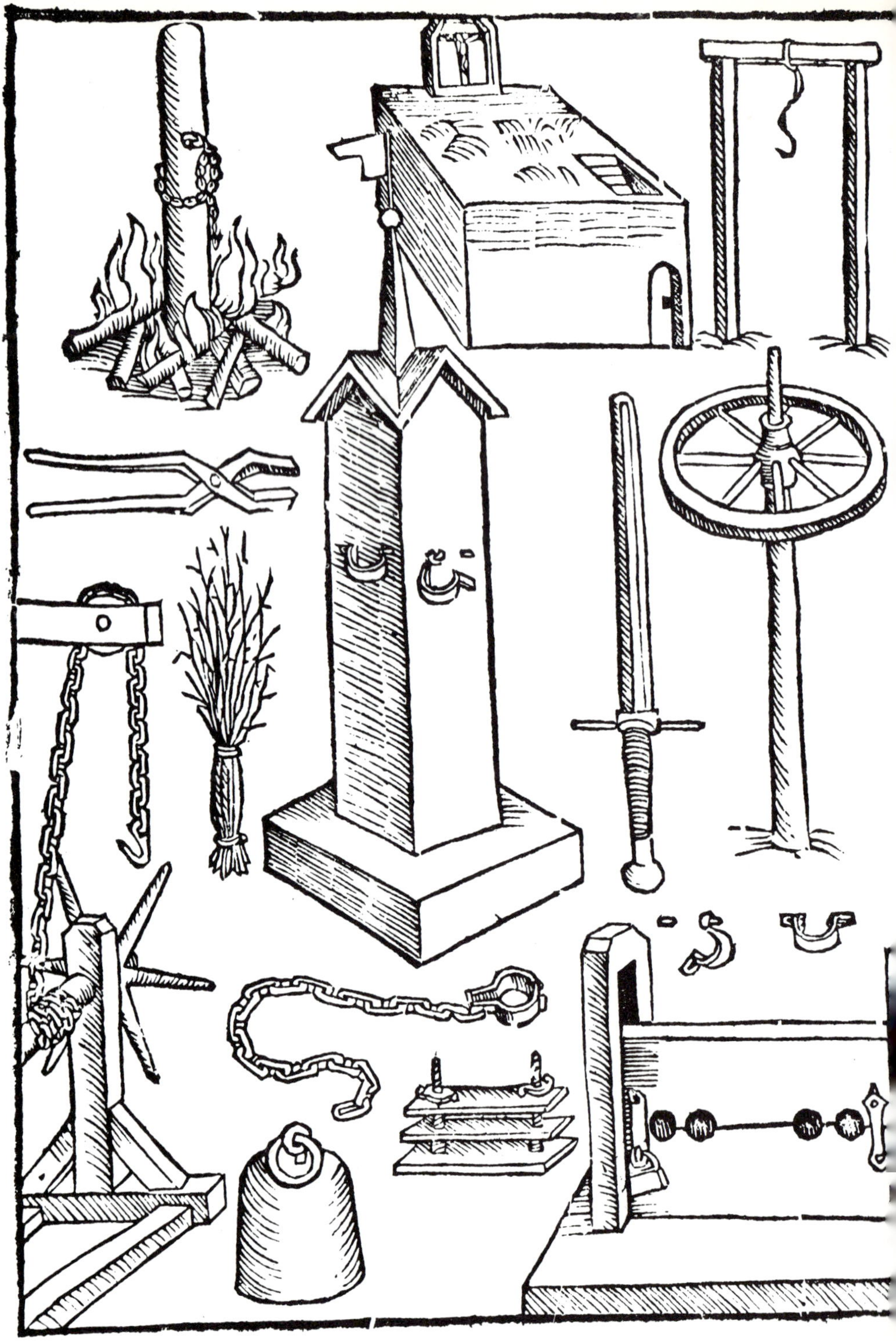

could confess it to the priest, and let those answer for it who compel me to do it . . . And so I made my confession, as follows, but it was all a lie.

"Now follows, dear child, what I confessed in order to escape the great anguish and bitter torture, which it was impossible for me to bear any longer.

(Here follows his confession, much as it appears in the minutes of his trial.)

Then I had to tell whom I had seen at the witch sabbat. I said that I had not recognized them. 'You old knave, I must put the torturer at your throat. Tell me, was not the Chancellor there?' So I said yes. 'Who besides?' I had not recognized anybody. So he said: 'Take one street after another. Begin at the market, go out on one street and back on the next.' I had to name several persons there. Then came the long street. I knew nobody. I had to name eight persons there. Then the Zinkenwert—one person more. Then over the upper bridge to the Georgthor, on both sides. Knew nobody again. Did I know nobody in the castle—whoever it might be, I should speak without fear. And thus continuously they asked me on all the streets, though I could not and would not say more. So they gave me to the torturer, told him to strip me and shave me all over, and put me to the torture. 'The rascal knows one on the marketplace, is with him every day, and yet he won't give his name.' By this they meant Burgomaster Dietmeyer, so I had to name him too.

"Then I had to tell what crimes I had committed. I said nothing . . . 'Hoist the knave up!' So I said that I was to kill my children, but I had killed a horse instead. It did not help. I had also taken a sacred wafer, and had buried it. When I said this, they left me in peace.

"Now, my dearest child, here you have all my acts and confession, for which I must die. And it is all sheer lies and inventions, so help me God. For all this I was forced to say through dread of torture beyond what I had already endured. For they never cease the torture till one confesses something. No matter how pious he is, he must be a witch. Nobody escapes, though he were an earl. If God sends no means of bringing the truth to light, our whole family will be burned. God in heaven knows that I know not the

Opposite Instruments of torture used in the Bamberg witch trials

Dress of condemned witches. *Left* of a witch who escaped burning by confessing before being sentenced, *middle* who confessed after being sentenced, and *right* who refused to confess

slightest thing. I die innocent and as a martyr.

"Dear child, keep this letter secret, so that no one finds it, or I shall be tortured most piteously and the jailers will be beheaded. So strictly is it forbidden . . . Dear child, pay this man a thaler . . . I have taken several days to write this—my hands are both crippled. I am in a sad plight . . .

"Good night, for your father Johannes Junius will never see you again (95)."

Terror in Germany

A parish priest from a village near Bonn spoke of the atmosphere of terror which prevailed in many parts of Germany in the early 1600s: "The victims of the funeral pyres are for the most part male witches. Half the city must be implicated, for already professors, law students, pastors, canons, vicars, and monks have been arrested and burned. His Princely Grace has seventy seminarians training to become priests, one of whom, eminent as a musician, was arrested yesterday; two others were sought, but have escaped. The Chancellor and his wife and the Private Secretary's wife have already been apprehended and executed.

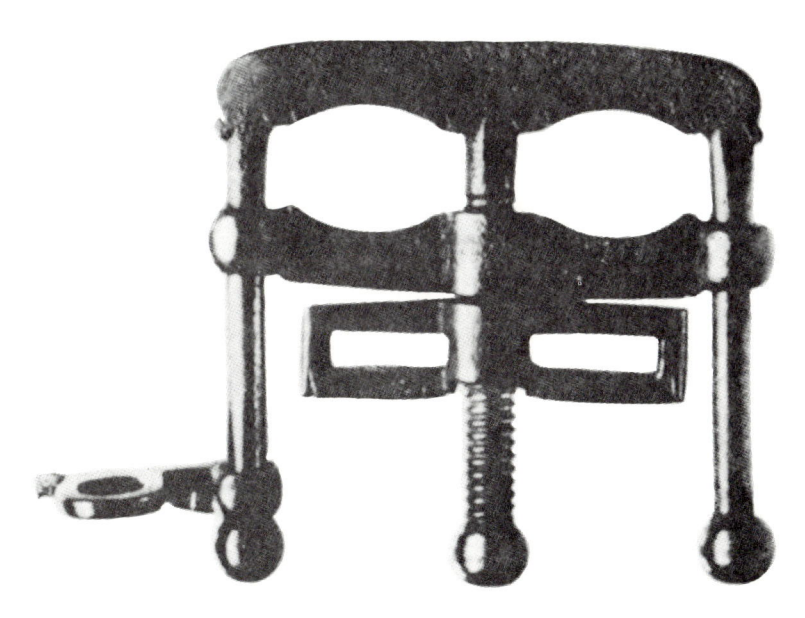

The pilliwinks, or thumbscrews, used in witch trials by the Scottish Privy Council

"On the Eve of our Lady's Day there was executed here a girl of nineteen who had the reputation of being the loveliest and most virtuous in all the city, and who from her childhood had been brought up by the Prince-Bishop himself. A canon of the cathedral, named Rotensahe, I saw beheaded and burned. Children of three or four years have devils for their paramours. Students and boys of noble birth, of nine, ten, eleven, twelve, thirteen, and fourteen years of age, have here been burned. To sum up, things are in such a pitiful state, that one does not know with what people one may talk and associate (96)."

Some people began to protest at the brutalities, including the Jesuit Heinrich Türck of Paderborn: "Some people began to feel great sympathy for the unfortunate victims; and grave doubts were raised as to whether the many persons who perished in the flames were really guilty and deserving of so horrible a death. In fact, many people thought that this treatment of human beings, who had been bought with the precious blood of Christ, was cruel and more than barbaric (97)."

Decline in witch hunts

After the 1600s, the fierce flame of persecution began to burn itself out. The persecutions in Bamberg, Germany, ended at the death of the Prince-Bishop in 1632; the city of Cologne had its last witchcraft execution in 1655. The last official execution in Germany did not, however, take place until as late as 1775, and the anti-witchcraft laws in Austria were not finally repealed until twelve years later. The witch trials in France began to decline in the early seventeenth century; although it took the extraordinary *chambre d'ardenté* affair of 1679–82 to finally expose the witchcraft delusion for what it was. (The star chamber of Louis XIV investigated widespread allegations of poisoning and witchcraft among the French nobility; a royal edict of 1682 denied the reality of witchcraft and sorcery). France's last execution for witchcraft took place in Lyons in 1745.

6 The English and Scottish Witch Trials

THE PERSECUTION of witches was far less violent in England than it was on the Continent. From 1542 to the last execution in 1684, only about a thousand deaths took place. There were various reasons for this. Perhaps the most important was that the Inquisition was never held in England. Under Henry VIII (1509–47) England had cut herself off from the Catholic church on the European continent. The English Channel, too, served as a natural barrier and defence against the importation of the worst barbarities. In Germany and France, there were mass executions of literally hundreds of witches at a time; the largest execution in England was of nineteen witches at Chelmsford in 1645, when the witchfinder-general, Matthew Hopkins, was at the peak of his power. And the execution of nine witches in Lancashire in 1612 was reckoned to be a very sensational event.

English opinion

Nor were the English courts as barbarous towards their victims as their counterparts on the Continent. Generally speaking, the only tortures used in England were bread and water diets, trussing of the limbs and enforced wakefulness. There were none of the brutalities of squassation, strappado, thumbscrews, and Spanish boots as used on the Continent (unless the alleged witchcraft was also considered to be treason). Also, witches in England were almost always hanged, not burned.

The start of the witchcraft persecution in England is marked by a statute against witchcraft, passed in the reign of Henry VIII in the year 1542. It enacted that if anyone should "use, devise, practise or exercise . . . any invocations or conjurations of spirits, witchcrafts, enchantments or sorceries, to find money or treasure, or to waste, consume or destroy any person in his body, members or goods ... or dig up or pull down any cross or crosses ... Then all and every such offence and offences ... shall be deemed accepted and adjudged felony. And that all and every person and persons offending as is abovesaid ... shall be deemed, accepted, and adjudged a felon and felons.

"And the offender and offenders contrary to this Act ... shall have and suffer such pains of death, loss and forfeitures of their lands, tenants, goods and chattels, as in case of felony [and] lose privilege of the clergy and sanctuary (98)."

Henry VIII's statute

The Statute of 1542 was also directed against any person who unlawfully conjured up spirits, and who "have made or caused to be made divers images and pictures of men, women, children, angels or devils, beasts or fowls, and also have made crowns, sceptres, swords, rings, glasses and other things, and giving faith and credit to such fantastical practices have digged up and pulled down an infinite number of crosses within this realm, and taken upon them to declare and tell where things lost or stolen should be become. Which things cannot be used and exercised but to the great offence of God's law, hurt and damage of the King's subjects, and loss of the souls of such offenders, to the great dishonour of God, infamy and disquietness of the realm (99)."

A similar statute was passed early in the reign of Queen Elizabeth I, in 1563. (The statute of Henry VIII had been repealed after his death in 1547, during the reign of Edward VI.) As the new statute explained: "At this present, there is no ordinary nor condign punishment provided against the practisers of the wicked offences of conjurations and invocations of evil spirits ... the which offences by force of a statute made in the XXXIII year of the reign of the late King Henry the Eighth were made to be felony, and so continued until the said statute was repealed by the Act and Statute of Repeal made in the first year of the reign of the late King Edward the VIth (100)."

Statute of Elizabeth I

Queen Elizabeth I may have been influenced by a sermon preached to her in 1560 by John Jewell, Bishop of Salisbury, to legislate against witches in 1563: "This kind of people (I mean witches and sorcerers), within these last few years are marvellously increased within Your Grace's realm. These eyes have seen most evident and manifest marks of their wickedness. Your Grace's subjects pine away even unto death, their colour fades, their flesh rots, their speech is benumbed, their senses are bereft. Wherefore, Your poor subjects' most humble petition unto Your Highness is, that the laws touching such malefactors may be put in due execution (101)."

Since the statute of Henry VIII had been repealed, "Many fantastical and devilish persons have devised and practised invocations and conjurations of evil and wicked spirits, and have used and practised witchcrafts, enchantments, charms and sorceries, to the destruction of the persons and goods of their neighbours and other subjects of this realm, and for other lewd intents and purposes contrary to the laws of Almighty God, to the peril of their own souls, and to the great infamy and disquietness of this realm (102)."

The statute of Elizabeth I now enacted once more that if any person should "use, practise, or exercise any invocations or conjurations of evil and wicked spirits, to or for any intent or purpose; or else if any person or persons after the said first day of June shall use, practise any witchcraft, enchantment, charm, or sorcery, whereby any person shall happen to be killed or destroyed . . . [then they] shall suffer pains of death as a felon or felons, and shall lose the privilege and benefit of sanctuary and clergy (103)." The wife and heir of any person convicted under the statute were however spared.

Death by hanging was the highest penalty which could be imposed for witchcraft—which in England was regarded more as a secular offence than a religious heresy. Other penalties were available, for example the pillory. If any person "shall use, practise, or exercise any witchcraft, enchantment, charm or sorcery, whereby any person shall happen to be wasted, consumed, or lamed in his or her body or whereby any goods or chattels of any person shall be destroyed, wasted, or impaired, then every such offender [shall] suffer imprisonment by the space of one whole year, without bail or mainprise, and once in every quarter of the said year, shall in some market town upon the market day . . . stand openly upon the pillory by the space of six hours, and there shall openly confess his or her error and offence (104)."

Penalties for witches

WITCHCRAFT IN ENGLAND AND SCOTLAND

1542 Statute of Henry VIII against witchcraft
1547 Repeal of statute of 1542 in reign of Edward VI
1563 Statute of Queen Elizabeth against witchcraft
1566 The first Chelmsford witch trials
1579 The Windsor witches; also the second Chelmsford trials
1582 St. Osyth Witches of Essex (case tried at Chelmsford)
1584 Publication of *Discovery of Witchcraft*, by the sceptic Reginald Scot
1589 Third Chelmsford witch trials
1593 Warboys witches of Huntingdon
1597 Publication of *Demonology* by James VI of Scotland (late James I of England)
1597 Case of the Burton Boy (Thomas Darling) in Staffordshire
1604 James I's statute against witchcraft
1604 Case of the Northwich Boy (an impostor)
1605 Abingdon witches and Anne Gunter (an impostor)
1612 Lancashire witch trials
1616 Case of the Leicester Boy (John Smith), an impostor
1620 Case of the Bilson Boy (William Perry), an impostor
1645 Case of the Faversham witches, Kent
Witchfinder-general Matthew Hopkins and the Chelmsford (or Manningtree) witch trials
1646 Death of Matthew Hopkins by tuberculosis
1647 Publication of *Discovery of Witches*, Matthew Hopkins
1649 Case of the St. Albans witches, Hertfordshire
1652 "Dr. Lamb's Darling": the trial of Anne Bodenham
Trial of the Wapping Witch (Joan Peterson) near London
1662 The Bury St. Edmunds witch trials
1674 Trial of Anne Foster at Northampton
1682 Trial of three Exeter Witches
1684 Last execution for witchcraft in England (Alice Molland at Exeter)
1712 Jane Wenham of Walkern in Herefordshire is last person convicted of witchcraft in England
1722 Last execution for witchcraft in Scotland
1736 Repeal of Statute of James I (1604)

In common with the law of the time, those of high rank were treated differently, even if accused of the same offences: "If such an offender shall happen to be a peer of this realm, then his trial therein to be had by his peers, as it is used in cases of felony or treason and not otherwise (105)."

Monarchy

A later statute of Elizabeth's reign, passed in 1581, was designed to protect the monarchy from witchcraft. If any person should "seek to know, and shall set forth by express words, deeds, or writings, how long her Majesty shall live or continue, or who shall reign as King or Queen of this realm of England after her Highness' decease [or] utter any manner of direct prophecies to any such intent or purpose [or] desire the death or deprivation of our sovereign lady the Queen's Majesty that now is or anything, directly to to the same effect. That then every such offence shall be felony, and therefore punishable by death and forfeiture (106)."

First Chelmsford Trial

The first major English witch trial took place at Chelmsford in Essex in 1566, soon after the passing of the Statute of 1563. The case was evidently considered an important one. On the first day it was tried by a local rector, the Reverend Thomas Cole, and Sir John Fortescue; and on the second by Sir Gilbert Gerard (the Attorney-General) and John Southcote, a Judge of the Queen's Bench Division. There were three defendants: Elizabeth Francis, Agnes Waterhouse and her daughter Joan Waterhouse. All three came from a small village near Chelmsford, called Hatfield Peveril. The trial is interesting, as it affords a good general picture of alleged witchcraft in England.

After endless questioning, Elizabeth Francis confessed to learning the art of witchcraft from her grandmother, Mother Eve, at the age of twelve. Mother Eve advised her to renounce God, "and to give of her blood to Satan (as she termed it), which she delivered her in the likeness of a white spotted cat, and taught her to call it by the name of Satan, and to keep it in a basket (107)."

Familiar spirit

Elizabeth soon began to ask the cat, her "familiar spirit," to do things for her. She asked "that she might be rich and have goods, and he promised her she should, asking her what she would like, and she said, 'Sheep' (for this cat spoke to her, as she confessed...) And this cat forthwith brought sheep into her pastures to the number of eighteen, black and white, which stayed with her for a time, but in the end they all wore away, she knew not how (108)."

Elizabeth then asked the cat to procure one Andrew Byles as her husband. Byles, a wealthy man, refused to marry her, however, and Elizabeth "willed Satan to waste his goods, which he forthwith did; and yet not being contented with this, she willed him to touch his body, which he forthwith did, and he died (109)."

After the death of Andrew Byles, Elizabeth began to look around for another marriage prospect. This was to be Francis, her husband at the time of the trial. "After they were married they lived quietly as she desired, being stirred, as she said, to much unquietness, and moved to swearing and cursing. And so she willed Satan her cat to kill the child, being about the age of a half year old—and he did so.

"And when she had still not found the quietness that she desired, she willed it to put a lameness in the leg of this Francis her husband. And it did, in this manner: it came in the morning to this Francis' shoe, and lay in it like a toad. And when he perceived it, putting on his shoe, and had touched it with his foot, he was suddenly amazed and asked her what it was. And she bade him kill it, and he was forthwith taken with a lameness of which he cannot be healed (110)."

Devil's mark   Having established to its own satisfaction that the cat was a devil, the court was very curious to discover Elizabeth's relationship with the cat Satan: Elizabeth confessed at her trial that "every time he did anything for her, she said that he required a drop of blood, which she gave him by pricking herself, sometimes in one place and then in another, Wherever she pricked herself there remained a red spot which was still to be seen (111)."

Elizabeth confessed to keeping her familiar for some fifteen or sixteen years. Finally she grew weary of him, and decided to part company with him. She "came to one Mother Waterhouse her neighbour, a poor woman, when she was going to the oven, and asked her to give her a cake. In return she would give her something that she should be the better for as long as she lived. And this Mother Waterhouse gave her a cake, whereupon she brought her this cat in her apron, and taught her just as she was taught before by her grandmother Eve, telling her that she must call him Satan and give him some of her blood, and bread and milk . . . (112)."

The third Chelmsford witch trials (1589). Joan Prentice is hanged as a witch

Typically, Elizabeth Francis made no mention of pacts with the devil himself, or sabbats and covenants. These things were seldom heard of in English witchcraft trials; they belonged to Europe with its deeper religious conflicts. But the familiar, and acts of *maleficium* (personal spite) were much more typical. Incidentally, the court relied entirely on Elizabeth's own confession in reaching a verdict of guilty. She was sentenced to twelve months' imprisonment. Some years later she was twice charged again with "bewitchment" and on the second occasion (1579) was hanged: not for heresy, it should be noted, but for causing personal injury.

Agnes Waterhouse

The second defendant in the Chelmsford trial was Mother Agnes Waterhouse. Questioned by the judges, Agnes Waterhouse confessed to working with the cat, Satan, just as Elizabeth Francis had done. For example, she perversely "willed him to kill one of her own hogs, which he did. And she gave him for his labour a chicken, which he first asked of her, and a drop of her blood. And this she gave him each time he did anything for her, by pricking her hand or face and putting the blood to his mouth. This he sucked, and at once would lie down in his pot again, in which she kept him. The spots of all these pricks are yet to be seen in her skin (113)."

Another time, Agnes told the court, she lost her temper with one Father Kersey. She was determined to punish him. She "took her cat Satan in her lap and put him in the wood before the door, and willed him to kill three of this Father Kersey's hogs. This he did, and returning again told her so, and she rewarded him as before, with a chicken and a drop of her blood. This chicken he ate up clean as he did all the rest, and she could find remaining neither bones nor feathers (114)."

No doubt under pressure, Agnes asked for a number of other acts of *maleficium* to be taken into account. She confessed that, "falling out with one Widow Goodday, she willed Satan to drown her cow and he did so, and she rewarded him as before. Also, when she fell out with another of her neighbours, she killed her three geese in the same manner.

"*Item*, she confessed that because she could have no rest, which she required, she caused Satan to destroy the brewing at that time. Also, being denied butter of another, she caused her to lose the curds two or three days after. *Item*, falling out with another of her neighbours and his wife, she willed Satan to kill him with the bloody flux, whereof he died, and she rewarded him as before (115)."

Finally, she confessed that "because she lived somewhat unquietly with her husband, she caused Satan to kill him, and he did so about nine years past, since which time she hath lived a widow (116)."

Metamorphosis

Satan now underwent a magic metamorphosis, it seemed, and became a toad. Agnes Waterhouse explained that "she kept the cat a great while in wool in a pot, and at length being moved by poverty to occupy [use] the wool, she prayed in the name of the Father and

The *Kingdom of Darkness* as portrayed on the title page of a book of the same name by Nathaniel Crouch (1688)

A witch and devils from the title page of *Daemonolatria* by Nicholas Remy (1693 edition)

of the Son and of the Holy Ghost that it would turn into a toad. And forthwith it was turned into a toad, and so she kept it in the pot without wool. Also she said that, going to Braxted a little before her apprehension, this Satan willed her to hie her home, for she should have great trouble, and that she should be either hanged or burned, shortly (117)." So ended Mother Waterhouse's confession. She was found guilty and so became the first person definitely known to have been hanged for witchcraft in England. Whether she had really experimented with magic, or was the victim of legal prejudice and local superstition, cannot be known. But her case undoubtedly influenced later ones, and began to confirm the impression that witchcraft was a rising social menace.

The third defendant at Chelmsford in 1566 was Mother Waterhouse's daughter, Joan Waterhouse, then a girl of eighteen. Joan was charged with bewitching a twelve-year-old girl, Agnes Brown who was "decrepit in her right leg and in her right arm." (In fact, she had probably suffered a stroke.) The only evidence against Joan was given by the girl herself, and was uncorroborated. Considering how many people were convicted on children's unsupported testimony in later years, Joan was lucky to be acquitted.

Joan Waterhouse

In the courtroom Joan told her accusers that she took little part in her mother's witchcraft, but that she once wished to frighten the girl Agnes Brown at Braxted, who had refused to give her some bread and cheese. Joan asked Satan what she must do. Satan demanded her body and soul. Joan, "being sore feared and desirous to be rid of him, said she would. And herewith he went to this girl in the likeness of an evil-favoured dog with horns on his head, and made her very much afeared, even now does haunt her (118)." The story about the dog was invented by the girl herself, Agnes Brown. Presumably the cat—or toad—had changed its appearance for the occasion!

The Chelmsford trials of 1566 attracted much notoriety in Elizabethan England. The county of Essex became famous for its witchcraft, and not surprisingly more cases of witchcraft were reported in the following years. The second major Chelmsford trials took place in 1579, when Elizabeth Francis was hanged. Two other people were hanged: Ellen Smith, whose mother had been hanged as a witch five years before, and Alice Nokes. Another defendant, Margery Stanton, was acquitted.

St Osyth witches Three years later, another notorious trial took place in Chelmsford, that of the St. Osyth witches. It was becoming routine by now to search the defendants' bodies for "witch marks" where the devil was supposed to have drunk their blood. It was also becoming routine to accept the testimony of highly imaginative and even hysterical children. A modern historian has commented: "The use of evidence in this trial would lead one to suppose that in England (in 1582) no rules of evidence were yet in existence. The testimony of children ranging in age from six to nine was eagerly received. No objection indeed was made to the testimony of a neighbour who professed to have overheard what he deemed an incriminating statement... Expert evidence was introduced in a roundabout way by the statement offered in court that a physician had suspected that a certain case was witchcraft. Nothing was excluded (119)."

Third Chelmsford trial The third major witch trial at Chelmsford took place in 1589, when one man and nine women were accused. Four of them were convicted and hanged. As before, the trials were characterized by children's unsupported evidence, imps, familiars, and petty acts of *maleficia*. There were no references to sabbats or pacts with the devil, as there were across the Channel in France and Germany. The persecution in Essex was to reach its peak in 1645, in the time of Matthew Hopkins, the witchfinder-general.

Law of James I In view of the apparent spread of witchcraft in the late 1500s, sterner laws were passed in 1604, the second year of the reign of James I. King James was himself an active student of witchcraft and author of *Demonology*, a book published in 1597. He personally believed in witchcraft and persecuted witches vigorously.

Death penalty In a speech given at Edinburgh in 1591, he reprimanded a jury for dismissing a charge of witchcraft: "For witchcraft, which is a thing grown very common amongst us, I know it to be a most abominable sin, and I have been occupied these three quarters of this year for the sifting out of them that are guilty herein. We are taught by the laws of both God and men that this sin is most odious. And by God's law punishable by death. By man's law it is called *maleficium* or *veneficium*, an ill deed or a poisonous deed, and punishable likewise by death.

"The thing that moved [the men of the assize] to find as they did, was that they had no testimony but of witches. By the civil law I know that such infamous persons are not received for witnesses, except in matters of heresy and *lesae majestatis*. For in other matters it is not thought meet, yet in these matters of witchcraft there is good reason that such be admitted. First, no honest person can know of these matters. Second, because they will not accuse themselves. Thirdly, because no act which is done by them can be seen.

"Further, I call those people witches who renounce God and yield themselves wholly to the Devil. But when they have recanted and repented, as these have done, then I account them not as witches, and so their testimony sufficient (120)."

James' 1604 statute made hanging mandatory for a first offence of witchcraft. This was so even if the offence did not amount to murder. If any man or woman "shall use, practise or exercise any invocation or conjuration of any evil and wicked spirit; Or shall consult, covenant with . . . or reward any evil and wicked spirit to or for any intent or purpose; Or take up any dead man, woman, or child out of his, her, or their grave . . . to be employed or used in any matter of witchcraft . . . whereby any person shall be killed, destroyed, wasted, consumed, pined, or lamed in his or her body . . . Then every such offender or offenders, their aiders, abettors, and counsellors, being of any the said offences duly and lawfully convicted and attainted, shall suffer pains of death as a felon or felons, and shall lose the privilege and benefit of clergy and sanctuary (121)."

It is interesting to see how James I's statute stressed the European idea of the covenant or pact with the devil. Perhaps English lawyers, scholars, and churchmen wanted to establish the idea that witchcraft was more than just an offence against man: but an offence against God. (The 1604 statute was eventually repealed in 1736 during the reign of George II.)

King James believed that witches could be tried by the ordeal by water, that is by "swimming" them. The accused person was thrown into a river or lake: if they floated they were guilty, if they sank, innocent. "God has appointed, for a supernatural sign of the monstrous impiety of the witches, that the water shall refuse to

Swimming witches

English villagers of the seventeenth century "swimming" an old woman suspected of being a witch

receive in her bosom those who have shaken off the sacred water of baptism and wilfully refused its benefit (122)."

Ordeal by water was an ancient method of determining innocence or guilt. This appeal to God's intervention had been known to the Babylonians. "If a man charges another with black magic and has not made good his case, the one who is thus taxed shall go to the river and plunge into the water. If the river overcomes him, his accuser shall possess his property. If, however, the river proves him innocent and he be not drowned, his accuser shall surely be put to death, and the dead man's property shall become the portion of him who underwent the ordeal (123)."

However, despite his earlier persecution of witches, James I (reigned 1603–25) began to change his opinions. He found that convictions were too often based on unreliable children's evidence. The cases which brought about his change of heart included the Abingdon trials of 1605, where the accusations were made by Anne Gunter, a girl of fourteen; the case of the Leicester Boy, John Smith, in 1618, whose testimony resulted in nine hangings; and a similar case two years later, that of the Bilson Boy, William Perry. A contemporary wrote: "The frequency of forged possessions [i.e. by devils] wrought such an alteration upon the judgement of King James that ... he grew first diffident of, and then flatly to deny, the workings of witches and devils as mere falsehoods and delusions (124)."

James I becomes sceptical

Indeed in the last nine years of his reign, it appears that only five people were hanged for witchcraft; and this was at a time when the executions in Bamberg, Germany, alone amounted to many hundreds.

Although there had by now been several well-publicized trials for witchcraft in England, notably at Chelmsford and in Lancashire in 1612, the worst single year of persecution was yet to come. This was 1645. For some years England had been the victim of religious extremism and civil war, and had developed a tradition of witch hunting. The moving spirit behind the persecution, which led to nineteen hangings, was Matthew Hopkins, an unsuccessful lawyer from Manningtree, Essex. Having failed as a lawyer Hopkins capitalized on local Puritan fears and prejudices by hunting out witches. Innocent, often unpopular people, became the victims of all the religious fears and frenzies of the locality; for this was a time of religious persecution not known since the Tudor troubles a century before.

Matthew Hopkins

Hopkins used the most ruthless methods open to him in securing convictions. One writer remarked: "Do but imagine a poor old creature, under all the weakness and infirmities of old age, set like a fool in the middle of a room, with a rabble of ten towns round about her house; then her legs tied cross, so that all the weight of her body might rest upon her seat. By that means, after some hours, the circulation of the blood would be much stopped, her sitting would be as painful as the wooden horse. Then she must continue in her pain four and twenty hours, without either sleep or meat, and since this was their ungodly way of trial, what wonder was it, if when they were weary of their lives, they confessed any tales that would please them, and many times they knew not what (125)."

Samuel Butler wrote of Matthew Hopkins (126):

And has not he, within a year,
Hanged three score of them in one shire?
Some only for not being drowned;*
And some for sitting above ground
Whole nights and days upon their breeches,
And feeling pain, were hanged for witches;
And some for putting knavish tricks
Upon green geese and turkey chicks,
Or pigs that suddenly deceased
Of griefs unnatural, as he guessed.

(*A reference to the ordeal by water.)

"Bewitchment" of people and animals was the common denominator of witches in England; and it was the charge most often levelled by Matthew Hopkins in the trials of 1645. Any passing reference by the accused to a small animal was taken to mean "imps"

Three witches, from a seventeenth-century English woodcut

or "familiars" given by the devil. A later writer commented: "My opinion is that when the witch finders had kept the poor people without meat or sleep till they knew not well what they said, then, to ease themselves of their tortures, they told them tales of their dogs and cats and kittens (127)."

Sometimes, teams of watchers would keep the accused awake for days and nights until they confessed to anything out of sheer exhaustion. And in the absence of witnesses, it was above all their confessions that their accusers wanted. As to one, John Lowes, they "kept him awake several nights together, and ran him backwards and forwards about the room until he was out of breath. Then they rested him a little and then ran him again. And thus they did for several days and nights together, till he was weary of his life and was scarce sensible of what he said or did (128)."

Witchfinder's methods

Working in this way, the self-styled witchfinder-general and his five or six assistants secured dozens of confessions, always on the flimsiest of pretexts. They began to receive commissions from other towns and villages near Chelmsford to root out the "witches" in their midst. Altogether, hundreds of people may have been hanged in the witch craze which swept the eastern counties.

In 1646, however, Hopkins began to meet his first critics. He had persecuted too fiercely and too widely. The popular support on which his campaign was based fell away. In 1646 he returned to his home in Manningtree and died of tuberculosis later that year.

But if the witchfinder-general had died, popular delusions had not. In the next few decades there were more deaths to come. In 1652, for example, six people were hanged at Maidstone in Kent. Ten years after that came the notorious Bury St. Edmunds Trials, improbably conducted by the great lawyer Sir Matthew Hale, later the Chief Justice. The trials were grotesque in reliance upon unsupported evidence, upon child impostors, and for their total disregard of basic rules of evidence, their sheer credulity.

Trials at Bury St Edmunds

At Bury St. Edmunds, much hostile evidence was given by some young children who claimed to be bewitched. Sir Thomas Browne was called to the trial to give evidence as a physician. Cautiously, he doubted whether the children were really bewitched: "His opinion was that the devil in such cases did work upon the bodies of men and women upon a natural foundation . . . For he conceived that

Matthew Hopkins, the witchfinder-general, presiding over the Chelmsford trials of 1645. The animals are the witches' familiars

these swooning fits were natural, and nothing else but that they call the mother [smother], but only heightened to a great excess by the subtlety of the devil, co-operating with the malice of these which we term witches, at whose instance he does these villainies (129)."

Many people, entirely innocent of witchcraft, suffered as a result of the hysterical condemnation of these Bury St. Edmunds children in 1662. Some of the children were in reality more prone to epileptic fits than to bewitchment. These included Deborah and Elizabeth Pacy, aged nine and eleven years, at Bury St. Edmunds.

"Their fits were various. Sometimes they would be less on one side of their bodies, sometimes on the other. Sometimes a soreness came over their whole bodies, so that they could not endure anyone to touch them. At other times they would be restored to the perfect use of their limbs and deprived of their hearing, at other times of their sight, at other times of their speech, sometimes for the space of one day, sometimes for two. And once they were wholly deprived of their speech for eight days together, and then restored to their speech again.

"At other times they would fall into swoonings, and when they recovered their speech they would cough extremely, and bring up much phlegm, and with it crooked pins, and once a twopenny nail with a very broad head. These pins, amounting to forty or more, together with the twopenny nail, were produced in court, with the affirmation of the said deponent that he was present when the said nail was vomited up, and also most of the pins. Commonly, at the end of every fit, they would cast up a pin, and sometimes they would have four or five fits in one day (130)."

The Bury St. Edmunds trials were the last of the major witch trials in England. After the Restoration of Charles II in 1660 executions were rare. Tolerance and social stability replaced the uncertain years of Puritanism and Civil War. The last execution for witchcraft in England was that of Alice Molland in Exeter in 1684, although other cases were tried later on. In 1712 Jane Wenham was the last person actually convicted of witchcraft; but she was reprieved. And in 1736, Parliament repealed the Act of 1604 in whose name the great English witch-hunt had been conducted.

An Oxford graduate, John Wagstaffe, was shocked at the wholesale executions for witchcraft which had taken place in England

and elsewhere. He wrote in the mid-seventeenth century: "I cannot think without trembling and horror on the vast numbers of people that in several ages and several countries have been sacrificed unto this cold opinion. Thousands, ten thousands, are upon record to have been slain, and many of them not with simple deaths, but horrid, exquisite tortures. And yet, how many are there more who have undergone the same fate, of whom we have no memorial extant (131)?"

Persecution in Scotland

If Wagstaffe was dismayed by the record in England, he must have been even more dismayed by the record in Scotland. Between 1573 and 1722 more than four thousand men, women and children were executed for witchcraft north of the border. "In no country did the witch-cult flourish more rankly, in no country did the belief persist more lately, in no country did the prosecution of sorcery rage fiercer and the fires blaze brighter than in Scotland. The lonely hills and untrod moors, the echoing glens and remote glades, seemed the very places for the hauntings of mysterious powers, influences which were, however, in popular law always ranged on the side of evil, harbingers of death and destruction and hell (132)."

As another writer has pointed out: "Scotland is second only to

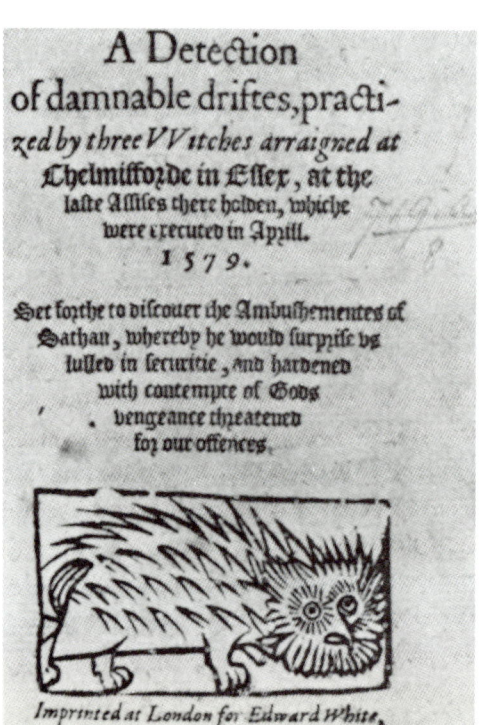

Title page of a pamphlet about the Chelmsford witch trials of 1579

Germany in the barbarity of its witch trials. The Presbyterian clergy acted like inquisitors and the church sessions often shared the prosecution with the secular law courts. The Scottish laws were, if anything, more heavily loaded against the accused. Finally, the devilishness of the torture was limited only by Scotland's backward technology in the construction of mechanical devices. Suppression of any opposition to belief in witchcraft was complete (133).''

The persecution in Scotland really began with the trial of the North Berwick witches in 1590. At this time, the witch craze in Scotland owed much of its momentum to the zealous support of James VI (later James I of England). Torture of the most savage kind was allowed, unlike in England. Accused persons could be and often were, convicted for "general reputation" of being witches, and not on their own confession; and convicted witches were not hanged, but burned (apparently to prevent the resurrection of the body).

North Berwick witches

In the worst cases, the brutality was appalling. Doctor Fian, alleged to be "a notable Sorcerer" and leader of the North Berwick witches, was burned for witchcraft in Edinburgh in January, 1591. He had undergone terrible bodily cruelty: "His nails upon all his fingers were riven and pulled off with an instrument called in Scottish a *Turkas*, which in England we call a pair of pincers, and under every nail there was thrust in two needles, even up to the heads. Despite these torments the doctor never shrunk any whit, neither would he then confess it the sooner, for all the tortures inflicted upon him.

"Then was he with all convenient speed ordered again to the torment of the boots, in which he remained a long time, and did abide so many blows in them, that his legs were crushed and beaten together as small as might be, and the bones and flesh so bruised that the blood and marrow spouted forth in great abundance, whereby they were made unserviceable forever (134)."

In Scotland, as elsewhere, informers were actively encouraged to denounce those they believed to be witches. "A hollow piece of wood or a chest is placed in the church into which anybody may freely cast a little scroll of paper, wherein may be contained the name of the witch, the time, place, and fact, *etc*. And the same chest, being locked with three several locks, is opened every fif-

Informers

teenth day by three inquisitors or officers appointed for that purpose, which keep three several keys. And thus the accuser need not be known, nor shamed with the reproach of slander or malice to his poor neighbour (135)."

Cost of Justice

Many Scottish towns and cities left gruesome records of the trials held in their districts. Some of them note the cost of trials and executions. This one comes from Kirkcaldy in 1636 (136):

	Pounds	Shillings	Pence
For ten loads of coal, to burn them, 5 marks or	3	6	8
For a tar barrel		14	0
For tows (*hangmans' rope*)		6	0
For hurden (*hemp fabric*) to be jumps (*short coats*) for them	3	10	0
For making of them		8	0
For one to go to Finmouth for the laird to sit upon their assize as judge		6	0
For the executioner for his pains	8	14	0
For his expenses here		16	4

Last Scottish trials

In Scotland, as on the continent of Europe, the worst atrocities were committed in the name of religion. The victims were searched for devil-marks or witch-marks which were supposed to prove the existence of the pact or covenant with the devil: the supreme heresy and crime against God.

Witch delusions persisted in Scotland until well into the eighteenth century. In 1704, for example, the Pittenweem witch trial on the east coast of Scotland provoked mob violence, condoned by the authorities, resulting in the deaths of two accused witches. In June, 1727, Janet Horne of Dornoch was burned for having used her daughter as a flying horse. As late as 1773, the Associated Presbytery formally reaffirmed its belief in witchcraft, a fearful tribute to the power of superstition only two hundred years ago.

7 The Salem Witch Trials

PERHAPS NO SINGLE witch hunt has attracted so much popular attention as that which took place at Salem in New England in the year 1692. This American witch hunt was remarkable not merely on account of the large number of people found guilty (Salem was a small community); but also because of the late date at which it took place. No one had been executed for witchcraft in England, for example, since 1684. But above all, the Salem affair has generally been seen as a fascinating microcosm of the whole Western witchcraft delusion.

Witchcraft in New England

Witchcraft had existed in New England many years before Salem. In 1656, for example, Anne Hibbins "was hanged for a witch only for having more wit than her neighbours. It was his very expression; she having, as he explained it, unhappily guessed that two of her persecutors, whom she saw talking in the street, were talking of her. This cost her her life, despite all he could do to the contrary, as he himself told us (137)." In other words, Anne Hibbins was the unfortunate victim of mere village gossip.

In New England, as elsewhere, hysteria was a common characteristic of the accusers. Cases of hysterical fits were known years before Salem. One such was that of Anne Cole in Hartford, Connecticut, in 1662: "Extremely violent bodily motions she many times had, even to the hazard of her life in the fears of those who saw them. And very often she gave great disturbance in the public worship of God to two other women, who had also strange fits. Once especially, on a day of prayer kept on that account, the motion and noise of the afflicted was so terrible that a godly person fainted at the appearance of it (138)." It was popularly imagined

Hysteria

that Anne Cole was bewitched, or possessed by devils. In the Puritan society of seventeenth-century America, the devil was every bit as real a person as God.

This hysteria, so often associated with witchcraft trials, has been the subject of much argument. Was it some kind of religious frenzy, or was it a medical condition? A modern writer has described medical hysteria as beginning "with a pain or a strange sensation situated at such or such a point of the body . . . it often begins in the lower part of the abdomen [and] seems to ascend and to spread to other organs. For instance, it very often spreads to the epigastrium, to the breasts, then to the throat. There it assumes rather an interesting form, which was for a very long time considered as quite characteristic of hysteria. The patient has the sensation of too big an object, as it were, a ball, rising in her throat and choking her (139)."

Cotton Mather

This medical description of hysteria has strong points of similarity with contemporary accounts. This one was given by the Boston minister Cotton Mather (1662–1728) in the case of the Goodwin children of Boston in 1688: "Sometimes they would be deaf, sometimes dumb, and sometimes blind, and often all this at once. One while their tongues would be drawn down their throats; another while they would be pulled out upon their chins to a prodigious length. They would have their mouths opened so wide that their jaws went out of joint, and they would at once clap together again with a force like that of a strong spring-lock.

"The same would happen to their shoulder blades, and their elbows, and hand wrists, and several of their joints. They would at times lie in a benumbed condition and be drawn together like those who are tied neck and heels, and presently be stretched out, yea, drawn backwards to such an extent that it was feared the very skin of their bellies would have cracked. They would make most piteous outcries that they were cut with knives, and struck with blows that they could not bear (140)."

A modern historian has written of Salem in 1692: "The primary causes should now be clear. There was an outbreak of epidemic hysteria in Salem Village which originated in experiments with the occult. And the hysterical hallucinations of the afflicted persons were confirmed by some concrete evidence of actual witchcraft

The Wonders of the Invisible World.

OBSERVATIONS

As well *Historical* as *Theological*, upon the NATURE, the NUMBER, and the OPERATIONS of the

DEVILS.

Accompany'd with,

I. Some Accounts of the Grievous Molestations, by DÆMONS and WITCHCRAFTS, which have lately annoy'd the Countrey; and the Trials of some eminent *Malefactors* Executed upon occasion thereof: with several Remarkable *Curiosities* therein occurring.

II. Some Counsils, Directing a due Improvement of the terrible things, lately done, by the Unusual & Amazing Range of EVIL SPIRITS, in Our Neighbourhood: & the methods to prevent the *Wrongs* which those *Evil Angels* may intend against all sorts of people among us; especially in Accusations of the Innocent.

III. Some Conjectures upon the great EVENTS, likely to befall, the WORLD in General, and NEW-ENGLAND in Particular; as also upon the Advances of the TIME, when we shall see BETTER DAYES.

IV A short Narrative of a late Outrage committed by a knot of WITCHES in *Swedeland*, very much Resembling, and so far Explaining, *That* under which our parts of *America* have laboured!

V. THE DEVIL DISCOVERED: In a Brief Discourse upon those TEMPTATIONS, which are the more Ordinary *Devices* of the Wicked One.

By **Cotton Mather**.

Printed by *Benj. Harris* for *Sam. Phillips*, 1693.

The title page of Cotton Mather's book of witchcraft *Wonders of the Invisible World* (1693)

and by many confessions, the majority of them also hysterical (141)."

But such explanations were foreign to New Englanders of the time. A sincere and devout man, Cotton Mather believed that witches must be fervently hunted down as evil monsters: "The devils, after a most preternatural manner, by the dreadful judgment of heaven, took a bodily possession of many people in Salem, and the adjacent places; and the houses of the poor people began to be filled with the horrid cries of persons tormented by evil spirits. There seemed to be an execrable witchcraft in the foundation of this wonderful affliction. Many persons, of divers characters, were accused, apprehended, prosecuted, upon the visions of the afflicted (142)." Cotton Mather was perhaps the most influential and active of the Massachusetts Bay Colony witch hunters.

Salem unrest It has been said of Salem: "The year 1692 seems to have been a particularly troubled one in New England. It was a time of political uncertainty, with Increase Mather at the English court, seeking clarification of the colony's government. The French were waging war, and the Indians were on the warpath. Taxes were intolerable (in 1691 the colonial government had demanded £1,346), the winter was cruel, pirates were attacking commerce, and smallpox was raging. In addition, the ingrown irritations of a small village, where ownership of land and boundaries were in dispute, increased the tensions. To men and women brought up in a restricting evangelical world, the troubles of 1692 were caused by the Devil (143)."

Religion A contemporary, John Hale, expressed the common fear of the people of Salem. The witches' "design was to destroy Salem Village, and to begin at the minister's house, and to destroy the Church of God, and to set up Satan's kingdom (144)." It has been pointed out that Massachusetts was not a monarchy or a republic, but a theocracy. Witchcraft—treason against God—was therefore treason against the state. Witchcraft seemed to threaten the very basis of the religious society in which the people of Salem lived: and the people of Salem took their religion very seriously.

Tituba In these circumstances, the local people were appalled to find that witchcraft was apparently being practised in the home of their minister, the Reverend Samuel Parris. Certain young women,

Cotton Mather

including his own daughter Elizabeth (aged nine) and her cousin Abigail Williams (aged eleven), used to spend their evenings with Tituba, the family's slave. Tituba would tell them lurid tales of the West Indies, filled with superstition which fired their ripe imaginations. Perhaps the girls were feverish or hysterical; perhaps they gave way to a terrible reaction against their strict Puritan background. Whatever the reality, to the people of Salem there could only be one explanation: witchcraft. The young girls, brought up in devout homes, were undeniably bewitched.

Elizabeth and Abigail deeply frightened their elders with their apparent bewitchment and they soon became the centre of local attention. Not surprisingly, they were joined by other impressionable girls, some of them rather older. The girls who indulged in this "sport," as it was called, included Elizabeth Parris, Abigail Williams, Ann Putnam (twelve), Elizabeth Hubbard (seventeen), Mary Walcott (sixteen), Elizabeth Proctor (twenty), Mercy Lewis (nineteen), Susan Sheldon (eighteen), Elizabeth Booth (eighteen) and others.

Childish spite

But if they were bewitched, who was responsible? In response to the earnest questions of the adults, the girls were quick to single out their unfortunate victims, perhaps out of fear of recanting, perhaps out of childish spite. The game had begun and must be played out to its terrible end. One by one the girls made their sworn depositions. Elizabeth Booth, for example, accused a neighbour, John Proctor: "The deposition of Elizabeth Booth, aged eighteen years, who testifieth and saith that since I have been afflicted, I have been most grievously tormented by my neighbour, John Proctor, senior, or his appearance [spectre]. Also I have seen John Proctor, senior, or his appearance [spectre] most grievously torment and afflict Mary Walcott, Mercy Lewis, and Ann Putnam, junior, by pinching, twisting, and almost choking them (145)."

On this "evidence," John Proctor was later convicted of witchcraft and hanged.

Similarly, Mary Walcott accused Abigail Faulkner of being a witch: "The deposition of Mary Walcott, who testifieth and saith that about the 9th August, 1692, I was most dreadfully afflicted by a woman that told me her name was Abigail Faulkner. But on the 11th of August, being the day of the examination of Abigail Faulkner, she did most dreadfully afflict me during the time of her examination. I saw Abigail Faulkner, or her appearance [spectre], most grievously afflict and torment Sarah Phelps and Ann Putnam. And I verily believe in my heart that Abigail Faulkner is a witch, and that she has often afflicted me and the aforesaid persons by acts of witchcraft (146)."

Adults' fears

It has been said that "there can be no mitigation of the crimes of the Salem girls. Never at any time, even during the hangings, was the slightest compunction or contrition shown, with the possible exception of Sarah Churchill and Mary Warren. They knew exactly what they were doing. Their acts during 1692 imply a state of utter delinquency, causing death without rhyme or reason, for sport. On 28th March, at Ingersoll's inn, one girl said she saw Mrs Proctor afflicting her. Mrs Ingersoll 'told the girl she told a lie, for there was nothing.' Then the girl said she did it for sport, 'They must have some sport.' (147).''

In the tense, unnatural atmosphere, virtually anything would be believed by the public. If witchcraft was the cause of the young peoples' conduct, then it must be ruthlessly eliminated—no matter who was implicated. The trouble was, that in the trials which were held late in 1692, the accusers were so anxious to locate the "guilty" parties, that elementary rules of evidence were ignored. The girls' imaginative evidence was believed almost entirely, and often without corroboration.

Worse still, even if a victim could prove an alibi, it was claimed that his "spectre" had appeared before the girls, and bewitched them. It seems extraordinary that any credence could be lent to this "spectral evidence" at so late a date. But it was a central part of the Salem trials, that a man could be condemned for what his "spectre" did. *Spectral evidence*

Cotton Mather believed in spectres, but did not think that spectral evidence should be admissible in court: "When there is not further evidence against a person but only this, that a spectre in their shape does afflict a neighbour, that evidence is not enough to convict the person of witchcraft. That the devils have a natural power which makes them capable of exhibiting what shape they please, I suppose nobody doubts. And I have no absolute promise of God that they shall not exhibit *mine*. It is the opinion, generally, of all Protestant writers that the Devil may thus abuse the innocent . . . (148)." But if Cotton Mather opposed spectral evidence, most people were only too willing to believe it, if the result was the desired conviction and punishment.

The Salem trials had much in common both with English and Continental witchcraft. The legend of flying witches, promoted by tradition, was confirmed by Mrs Anne Foster at the Salem trials: "She and Martha Carrier did both ride on a stick or pole when they went to the witch meeting at Salem Village, and that the stick broke as they were carried in the air above the tops of the trees, and they fell. But she did hang fast about the neck of Goody Carrier and *Flying witches*

A woman seized by a hysterical fit, probably like that experienced by the Salem girls

were presently at the village, that she was then much hurt of her leg (149)."

Maleficium

Other evidence mentioned familiars, bewitchment, acts of *maleficium* or petty spite such as killing pigs, and possession by devils. One or two of the girls even claimed to have seen the accused writing their names in the "devil's book," but the Salem magistrates were unwilling to believe in this, at least.

Increase Mather

Increase Mather (1639–1723)—the President of Harvard—was one New Englander to advise caution: "It were better that ten suspected witches should escape than that one honest person should be condemned ... It is better a guilty person should be absolved, than that he should without ground of conviction be condemned. I had rather judge a witch to be an honest woman, than judge an honest woman as a witch (150)." But his advice was scarcely heeded; and in any case he believed in witchcraft as much as anyone.

Salem prisoners

The trials continued. The depositions of the girls were taken, the spectral evidence believed; the religious fears of the Puritan community inflated. Dozens of victims were thrown into jail. The Salem

A house at Salem in the late seventeenth century

prisoners were badly treated: "An especially shocking detail about these trials is that the accused had to pay for their maintenance in jail, even when acquitted! A reprieve cost a fee, a discharge another. The relatives paid the hangman's fee for the execution. Many remained in prison after the general jail delivery because their possessions had been sold to maintain their families in the meantime. Sarah Dustin was acquitted in January, 1693, but, having no one to come to her aid, died in prison. Margaret Jacobs was acquitted, but the property of her parents had been seized, and she was kept in jail until at length a generous stranger (a Mr Gammon) heard of her plight and bought her freedom. William Buckley spent his last shilling paying £10 to release his wife and daughter (151)."

Some of the Salem "witches" deeply impressed the crowd at their executions: "They protested their innocence as in the presence of the great God whom forthwith they were to appear before. They wished, and declared their wish, that their blood might be the last innocent blood shed upon that account. With great affection [emotion] they entreated Mr Cotton Mather to pray with them.

Executions

They prayed that God would discover that witchcrafts were among us. They spoke without reflection on jury and judges for bringing them in guilty and condemning them.

"They prayed earnestly for pardon for all other sins and for an interest in the precious blood of our dear Redeemer. They seemed to be very sincere, upright, and sensible of their circumstances on all account, especially Proctor and Willard, whose whole management of themselves from the jail to the gallows and whilst at the gallows was very affecting and melting to the hearts of some considerable spectators . . . (152)."

Another victim, the Reverend George Burroughs, was obviously innocent: "Mr Burroughs was carried in a cart with the others through the streets of Salem to execution. When he was upon the ladder he made a speech for the clearing of his innocence, with such solemn and serious expressions as were to the admiration of all present. His prayer (which he concluded by repeating the Lord's Prayer) was so well worded, and uttered with such composedness, and such (at least seeming) fervency of spirit, as was very affecting and drew tears from many. Indeed, it seemed to some that the spectators would hinder the execution (153)." Burroughs was hanged on 19th August, 1692.

But despite scenes such as this, the superstition at Salem in 1692 seemed indestructible. At the execution of Samuel Wardwell on 22nd September, 1692, "while he was speaking to the people protesting his innocence, the executioner was at the same time smoking tobacco, and the smoke coming in his face interrupted his discourse; those accusers said the Devil hindered him with smoke (154)."

All in all, the toll of Salem, a township of a hundred-odd households, was enormous. "During the hysteria, almost 150 people were arrested. A search of all the court records would no doubt add to this number. Because of the time taken to convict each prisoner, only thirty-one were tried in 1692, not including Sarah Churchill and Mary Warren, two accusers who briefly recanted. The court of Oyer and Terminer (hear and determine) sentenced to death all thirty-one, of whom six were men. Nineteen were hanged. Of the remaining twelve, two (Sarah Osborne and Ann Foster) died in jail; one (Giles Cory) was pressed to death; one (Tituba) was held indefinitely in jail without trial. Two (Abigail Faulkner and Elizabeth Proctor) postponed execution by pleading pregnancy and lived long enough to be reprieved. One (Mary Bradbury) escaped from jail after sentencing; and five made confessions which secured reprieves for them (155)."

The historian George Lincoln Burr declared that "the New England panic at Salem was but a last bright flicker of the ghastly glare which had so long made hideous the European night (156)." Another great student of witchcraft wrote of the Salem witch hunt: "Error is seldom overthrown by mere reasoning. It yields only to the logic of events. No power of learning or wit would have rooted the witchcraft superstition out of the minds of men. Nothing short of a demonstration of their deformities, follies, and horrors, such as here was held up to the view of the world, could have given their death blow. This was the final cause of Salem witchcraft, and makes it one of the great landmarks in the world's history (157)."

A last bright flicker

Opposite The slave Tituba telling West Indian tales to the Salem children

Epilogue

THE GREAT EUROPEAN witch hunt, which lasted roughly from 1450 to 1750, is one of the strangest phenomena in the history of the West. It is remarkable not only because of the large number of victims whom it claimed, some 100,000, in every European state. It was remarkable above all in that it coincided with the start of the European renaissance. In the fifteenth century the towns were growing and prospering and asserting their independence from old forms of feudalism. Learned men were revitalizing old sciences of physics, chemistry, mathematics and astronomy, drawing their inspiration from ancient Greece and the Arab world. Printers were mass-producing books and pamphlets on all subjects under the sun for the new generation, with titles on philosophy, rhetoric, grammar, theology, the sciences and mathematics, agriculture, building and countless other subjects. And yet it was the most educated and apparently rational men who everywhere lent their support to the witch craze. They were men like the French philosopher Jean Bodin, famous bishops and lawyers, and kings like James I of England. If this seems strange to a modern reader, one should reflect that brutally irrational purges were not the sole preserve of old Europe. The twentieth century has seen the relentless persecution of one people, the Jews, six million of whom lost their lives to racist prejudices; it has seen the consistent repression of racial minorities since 1945; and Americans have experienced the political horror of McCarthyism, very aptly called a "witch hunt." Human conduct is never as rational as many people believe. Nor, unfortunately, is it as guided by common humanity and tolerance as it might be.

Glossary

AMULET Object worn as a magical charm, e.g. a bracelet or necklace.
ASTROLOGY The art of predicting human affairs by the study of the stars.
BENEFICIUM Benefit, especially as conferred by a white witch.
BEWITCHMENT Enchantment by a witch.
BLACK MASS Blasphemous parody of the Catholic mass.
CONJURE To invoke or summon, as to conjure up evil spirits.
COVEN Cell of witches.
DEVIL'S MARK Sign placed by the devil on the body of a witch (usually a birthmark or scar).
EVIL EYE Hostile stare able to bewitch.
EXORCISM Expulsion of devil from a person or place.
FAMILIAR *or* FAMILIAR SPIRIT Demon or imp in form of a small animal given to a witch by the devil for small errands.
GOETY Black magic practised with the help of evil spirits.
HERESY Religious unorthodoxy, once punishable by death.
INCUBUS Evil male spirit supposed to seduce sleeping women at night.
INQUISITION Tribunal of the Holy Office founded in 1199 to expose and punish religious unorthodoxy.
LUCIFER Another name for Satan.
LYCANTHROPY Change to sadistic animal form, especially at night (e.g. werewolves).
MALEFICIUM Harm or evil caused by witches.
METAMORPHOSIS A change of physical form (e.g. the *Golden Ass* of Apuleius).
NECROMANCY Prediction, or discovery of hidden things, with the aid of the dead.

PHILTRE Potion.

PILLIWINKS Instrument of torture for crushing fingers.

POLTERGEIST Noisy mischievous thieving spirit.

POSSESSION Inhabiting of a person's body by the devil (usually against their will).

SABBAT(H) Blasphemous parody of the mass and other Christian rites.

SPECTRAL EVIDENCE Testimony that although a real person had not been seen performing some act, his spectre had been seen doing it. Where spectral evidence was allowed, a man was held responsible for what his spectre was supposed to have done.

SQUASSATION Extreme form of strappado, using heavy weights.

STRAPPADO Form of torture based on sudden dropping of the body from ropes.

STRIGES Witches supposed to take the form of screech owls.

SUCCUBUS Evil female spirit supposed to seduce sleeping men at night.

THEURGY White magic practised with the help of angels and prayers to God.

TRANSVECTION Magical flight from one place to another, e.g. on broomsticks or straws.

Further Reading

Burr, George Lincoln, *Narratives of the Witchcraft Cases 1648-1706* (Barnes & Noble, Inc., New York, 1914). Classic study by a great American scholar.

Davies, Reginald Trevor, *Four Centuries of Witch Beliefs* (Methuen, London, 1947). An important general survey of English witchcraft.

Hansen, Chadwick, *Witchcraft at Salem* (Hutchinsons, London, 1970; New American Library, New York, 1970). A thorough and well-documented account.

Lochhead, M., *Magic and Witchcraft of the Borders* (Hale, 1984)

Pennick, *Witchcraft in New England: An Investigation* (Wolf Publications, 1976)

Robbins, Rossell Hope, *The Encyclopedia of Witchcraft and Demonology* (Spring Books, London, 1959; Crown Publishers, New York, 1959). A graphic and thorough reference tool with a thousand-entry bibliography.

Rosen, Barbara (ed.), *Witchcraft* (Edward Arnold, London, 1969). Valuable reprints of original Elizabethan and Jacobean source material heavily annotated.

Ross, S., *Spotlight on Medieval Europe* (Wayland, 1986)

Seth, Ronald, *In the Name of the Devil: Great Scottish Witchcraft Cases* (Jarrolds, London, 1969; Walker & Co., New York, 1970). Popular account.

Starkey, Marion, *The Devil in Massachusetts* (Robert Hale, London, 1949; Knopf Inc., New York, 1949). A dramatic reconstruction of the Salem affair.

Summers, Montague, *Geography of Witchcraft* (University Books, Inc., New York, 1958). A classic study, if slightly dated in the light of more recent work.

Trevor-Roper, H. R., *The European Witch Craze of the 16th and 17th Centuries* (Pelican, London, 1969). A scholarly approach towards an understanding of the witch craze.

Notes on Sources

(1) William Shakespeare, *A Midsummer Night's Dream* (1594)
(2) R. Burton, *Anatomy of Melancholy* (1652)
(3) Arthur Wilson, *Account of his Life* (1779)
(4) John Heinrich Zopft, *Dissertatio de Vampiris Serviensibus* (1733)
(5) Reginald Scot, *The Discoverie of Witchcraft* (1584)
(6) Bishop Samuel Harsnett, *Declaration of Popish Impostures* (1599)
(7) Papal Bull, *Summis desiderantes affectibus* (1484) issued by Pope Innocent VIII
(8) *Ibid*
(9) Papal Bull, *Cum acceperimus* (1501)
(10) *Exodus xxii*: 18
(11) *Leviticus xix*: 31
(12) *Isaiah viii*: 19
(13) *Leviticus xx*: 27
(14) Bernard of Clairvaux
(15) Francesco-Maria Guazzo, *Compendium Maleficarum* (1608)
(16) William West, *Simboleography* (1594)
(17) Gratian, *Decretum*
(18) King James VI of Scotland, *Preface to Dæmonologie* (1597)
(19) King James VI of Scotland, Speech at Edinburgh (June, 1591)
(20) Francesco-Maria Guazzo, *Compendium Maleficarum* (1626 edition)
(21) Thomas Ady, *A Candle in the Dark* (1656)
(22) Thomas Hobbes, *Leviathan* (1651)
(23) Edmund Spenser, *The Faerie Queene* (1590)
(24) R. Bovet, *Pandemonium* (1684)
(25) Thomas Potts, *The Wonderfull Discoverie of Witches* (1613)
(26) Reginald Scot, *The Discoverie of Witchcraft* (1584)
(27) Samuel Harsnett, *Declaration of Popish Impostures* (1599)
(28) Reginald Scot, *The Discoverie of Witchcraft* (1584)
(29) *Ibid*
(30) William Rowley, Thomas Dekker & John Ford, *The Witch of Edmonton*, Act V (1658)
(31) Ludovico Sinistrari, *De Demonialitate* (first modern edition, Paris, 1879)
(32) Jacques Fontaine, *Des Marques des Sorciers* (1611)
(33) R. H. Robbins, *Encyclopaedia of Witchcraft and Demonology* (1959)
(34) Sir George Mackenzie, *Laws and Customs of Scotland* (1678)
(35) Francesco-Maria Guazzo, *Compendium Maleficarum* (1626 edition)
(36) Johannes Nider, *Formicarius* (c. 1435)
(37) Trial account of Isobel Gowdie, Scotland (1662)
(38) Francesco-Maria Guazzo, *Compendium Maleficarum* (1608); translated by Dr R. H. Robbins
(39) *The Apprehension and Confession of Three Notorious Witches... in the County of Essex* (1589)
(40) *Doctor Lamb's Darling* (1653)
(41) William Shakespeare, *A Comedy of Errors*, Act IV, Sc. III
(42) Francesco-Maria Guazzo, *Compendium Maleficarum* (1626 edition)
(43) Proceedings of the trial of Isobel Gowdie, Scotland (1662)
(44) Thomas Middleton, *The Witch*
(45) Ben Jonson, *The Masque of Queenes*
(46) *News from Scotland* (1591)
(47) *Ibid*
(48) Quoted in *The Encyclopedia of Witchcraft and Demonology* (1959), page 317
(49) Rendered into modern English by R. Seth, *In the Name of the Devil* (1969)
(50) Francesco-Maria Guazzo, *Compendium Maleficarum* (1626)
(51) *Ibid*
(52) Quoted in *The Encyclopedia of Witch-*

craft and Demonology (1959), page 421
(53) Quoted by R. Seth, *In the Name of the Devil* (1969)
(54) Henry More, *An Antidote against Atheism* (1653)
(55) Trial of Isobel Gowdie, Scotland, 1662
(56) Quoted by R. Seth, *In the Name of the Devil* (1969)
(57) *Ibid*
(58) Casper Pencer, *Commentarius* (1560)
(59) Francesco-Maria Guazzo, *Compendium Maleficarum* (1626)
(60) Proceedings of the trial of Isobel Gowdie, Scotland, 1662
(61) *Ibid*
(62) Candidus Brognolus Bergomensi, *Manuale Exorcistarum* (1651)
(63) *Wonderful Discovery of Witches in the County of Lancashire* (1613)
(64) Trial proceedings of Isobel Gowdie, Scotland, 1662
(65) *Ibid*
(66) Francesco-Maria Guazzo, *Compendium Maleficarum* (1626)
(67) Chelmsford witch trials, 1616
(68) Recited by James Device in the Lancashire witch trials of 1612
(69) Quoted by R. Seth, *In the Name of the Devil* (1969)
(70) Trial of Isobel Gowdie in 1662; quoted by R. Seth, *In the Name of the Devil* (1969)
(71) *Ibid*
(72) *Ibid*
(73) William Perkins, *A Discourse of the Damned Art of Witchcraft* (1608)
(74) Richard Eden, *History of Travel in the West and East Indies* (1577)
(75) Francesco-Maria Guazzo, *Compendium Maleficarum* (1626)
(76) Rendered into modern English by R. Seth, *In the Name of the Devil* (1969)
(77) Vincentius von Berg, *Enchiridium*
(78) *Ibid*
(79) Rendered into modern English by R. Seth, *In the Name of the Devil* (1969)
(80) Vincentius von Berg, *Enchiridium*
(81) Robert Herrick, *A Mocking View of Exorcism*
(82) R. H. Robbins, *The Encyclopedia of Witchcraft and Demonology* (1959)
(83) Bernardus Guidonis, *The Inquisitor's Manual* (First modern edition Paris, 1886)
(84) Quoted by R. H. Robbins, *The Encyclopedia of Witchcraft and Demonology* (1959)
(85) Friedrich von Spee, *Cautio Criminates* (1631)
(86) Jean Bodin, *Démonomanie* (1580)
(87) *Malleus Maleficarum* (1486)
(88) Philip Limborch, *History of the Inquisition* (1692)
(89) Friedrich von Spee, *Cautio Criminalis* (1631)
(90) *Ibid*
(91) Francesco-Maria Guazzo, *Compendium Maleficarum* (1626 edition)
(92) Johan Lindon, *History of Treves*
(93) Cornelius Agrippa, *De Incertitudine et Vanitate Scientiarum* (1531)
(94) R. H. Robbins, *The Encyclopedia of Witchcraft and Demonology* (1959)
(95) Letter of Johannes Junius, dated 24th July, 1628
(96) Quoted in R. H. Robbins, *The Encyclopedia of Witchcraft and Demonology* (1959)
(97) *Ibid*
(98) *Statutes of the Realm*, vol. iii, p. 837
(99) *Ibid*
(100) *Statutes of the Realm*, vol. iv, p. 446
(101) Sermon of Bishop John Jewell of Salisbury (1560)
(102) *Statutes of the Realm*, vol. iv, p. 446
(103) *Ibid*
(104) *Ibid*
(105) *Ibid*
(106) *Ibid*
(107) *The Examination and Confession of Certain Witches at Chelmsford* (1566)
(108) *Ibid*
(109) *Ibid*
(110) *Ibid*

(111) *Ibid*
(112) *Ibid*
(113) *Ibid*
(114) *Ibid*
(115) *Ibid*
(116) *Ibid*
(117) *Ibid*
(118) *Ibid*
(119) Wallace Notestein, *History of Witchcraft in England* (1911)
(120) King James VI of Scotland, Tolbooth Speech (1591)
(121) *Statutes of the Realm*, vol. iv, part 2, p. 1028
(122) James I, *Demonologie* (1597)
(123) Code of Hammurabai King of Babylon, third millennium B.C.
(124) Dr. Thomas Fuller, *Church History of Britain* (1655)
(125) Bishop Francis Hutchinson, *Historical Essay Concerning Witchcraft* (1718)
(126) Samuel Butler, *Hudibras* (1664)
(127) Bishop Francis Hutchinson, *An Historical Essay Concerning Witchcraft* (1718)
(128) *Ibid*
(129) *A Trial of Witches* (1682)
(130) *Ibid*
(131) John Wagstaffe, *The Question of Witchcraft Debated* (1669)
(132) Montague Summers, *The Geography of Witchcraft* (1927)
(133) R. H. Robbins, *The Encyclopedia of Witchcraft and Demonology* (1959)
(134) *News from Scotland, Declaring the Damnable Life and Death of Doctor Fian* (1591)
(135) Reginald Scot, *Discovery of Witchcraft* (1584)
(136) R. H. Robbins, *The Encyclopedia of Witchcraft and Demonology* (1959)
(137) William F. Poole, "Witchcraft in Boston," *Memorial History of Boston* (1881)
(138) *Massachusetts Historical Society Collections* 4th Series, viii, page 466
(139) Pierre Janet, *The Major Symptoms of Hysteria* (New York, 1907)
(140) Cotton Mather, *Memorable Providences*
(141) Chadwick Hansen, *Witchcraft at Salem* (1970)
(142) Cotton Mather, *Diary*, ed. Worthington C. Ford, Boston (1911)
(143) R. H. Robbins, *The Encyclopedia of Witchcraft and Demonology* page 429 (1959)
(144) John Hale, *A Modest Inquiry into Witchcraft*, Boston (1702)
(145) Deposition of Elizabeth Booth at Salem (1692)
(146) Deposition of Mary Walcott at Salem (1692)
(147) R. H. Robbins, *The Encyclopedia of Witchcraft and Demonology* (1959)
(148) Cotton Mather, letter to John Foster dated 17th August, 1692
(149) R. H. Robbins, *The Encyclopedia of Witchcraft and Demonology* (1959)
(150) Increase Mather, in an address to Boston ministers in 1692
(151) R. H. Robbins, *The Encyclopedia of Witchcraft and Demonology* (1959)
(152) Letter of Thomas Brattle, quoted in Chadwick Hansen, *Witchcraft in Salem* (1970)
(153) George Lincoln Burr, *Narratives of the Witchcraft Cases 1648–1706* (New York, 1914)
(154) Robert Calef (1700)
(155) R. H. Robbins, *The Encyclopedia of Witchcraft and Demonology* (1959)
(156) George Lincoln Burr, *The Literature of Witchcraft* (1890)
(157) Charles W. Upham, *Salem Witchcraft* (1867)

Index

Ady, Thomas, 24
Amulets, 29, 53, 55, 71, 121
Aschhausen, Prince-Bishop Johann von, 78-81, 85, 86
Auldearne, 32, 41, 42, 43

Bamberg, 78, 79, 86, 101
Banquets, witches', 43, 45, 69
Baptism, 14, 31, 32, 100
Barker, Susan, 54
Bernard of Clairvaux, 16
Bewitchment, 51-54, 58, 60-61, 93, 97, 102, 103, 105, 110, 113, 114, 116, 121
Bible, the, 16, 24
Bilson Boy, case of the, 101
Black sabbaths; see Sabbats
Bodenham, Anne, 35
Bodin, Jean, 64, 71, 120
Bribery, 75, 78
Brodie, Margaret, 32, 43
Butler, Samuel, 102

Carolina Code, 63
Catholicism, 13, 24, 31, 32, 54, 61, 63, 87
Charms; see Spells and Amulets
Christian, 24, 31, 32, 56, 61, 62, 64, 72
Church, the; see Catholicism
Clergy, 12, 23, 26, 41, 53, 54, 62, 64, 66, 75, 78, 81, 84, 85, 88, 99, 102, 107, 112
Corpses, 21, 37, 48, 49, 54
Covens, 31, 36, 41, 45, 49, 50, 121

Demonology, 21, 98
Demonomanie, 64
Device, Elizabeth, 25
Devil marks, 24, 28, 29, 30, 34, 70, 92, 94, 98, 108, 121
Devil, the; see Satan
Devils (demons), 11, 12, 13, 16, 18-19, 21, 23, 25, 26, 27, 28, 41, 43, 45, 61, 69, 70, 88, 115, 116
Drummond, Alexander, 55
Duncan, Gillis, 40

Edinburgh, 55, 98, 107
Edmonton, Witch of, 27-28

Edward VI, 88
Elizabeth I, 19, 88, 89, 91
England, 22, 25, 87, 91, 97, 98, 101, 102, 105, 108, 109
Essex, 97, 98, 101
Europe, 11, 15, 24, 28, 31, 49, 61, *Ch. 5*, 87, 93

Familiars, 16, 20, 21, 25, 31, 91, 92, 94, 97, 98, 103, 116, 121
Fian, Dr., 37, 107
Flying witches, 21, 24, 36, 37, 70, 115, 121
Flying ointment, 36-37, 70
Fontaine, Jacques, 28
France, 41, 63, 67, 69, 86, 87, 98, 112
Francis, Elizabeth, 91, 92, 93, 94, 97

George II, 99
Germany, 13, 36, 58, 63, 66, 69, 78, 84, 86, 87, 98, 101, 107
Gowdie, Isobel, 32, 36, 41, 45, 48, 49, 50, 58
Guazzo, Francesco-Maria, 16, 30, 32, 51, 58, 61, 74

Henry VIII, 87, 88, 89
Heresy, 13, 15, 23, 24, 31, 54, 63, 64, 68, 69, 75, 89, 93, 99, 108, 121
Hobbes, Thomas, 24
Hopkins, Matthew, 87, 98, 101, 102, 103
Hubbard, Elizabeth, 114
Hysteria and fits, 54, 98, 105, 109, 110, 113

Incubus, 12, 13, 69, 70, 121
Inquisition, the, 12, 46, 63, 64, 67, 68, 69, 73, 78, 87, 121
Inquisitors, 14, 15, 64, 66, 74, 75, 78, 107
Italy, 15, 36, 43, 61, 63, 69, 78

James (I of England and VI of Scotland), 21, 22, 37, 40, 98, 99, 100-101, 107, 120

Jonson, Ben, 37
Junius, Johannes, 79, 81, 83, 84

Leicester Boy, case of the, 101
Lewis, Mercy, 114
Louis XIV, 86
Lycanthropy, 49, 121

Maleficium, 21, 22, 41, 50, 51, 93, 94, 98, 116, 121
Malleus Maleficarium, 63, 71
Martin, Joan, 42
Mather, Cotton, 110, 112, 115, 117
Metamorphosis, 48, 49, 94, 121
Middleton, Thomas, 37
More, Henry, 45

New England, 109, 112, 119
New World, the, 31, *Ch. 7*

Ointment, magic, 54, 70

Pacts with the devil, 27, 31, 32, 34, 35, 36, 41, 45, 47, 50, 63, 93, 98, 99, 108
Papal bulls, 12-15, 24, 63, 67
Parris, Elizabeth, 113, 114
Poltergeists, 11, 122
Popes, Alexander VI, 15; Innocent IV, 64, 67, 69; Innocent VIII, 12; Pius VII, 68
Prentice, Joan, 34, 35
Pricking of witches, 29-30
Protestantism, 31, 63, 115
Proctor, Elizabeth, 114, 119
Punishments for witchcraft, 14, 16, 22, 23, 46, 63, 89, 97, 98, 99, 107, 114, 115
Puritanism, 105, 113, 116
Putnam, Anne, 114

Sabbats, 36, 37, 40, 41, 43, 45, 47, 58, 69, 83, 93, 98, 121
Salem, *Ch. 7*
Satan, 12, 21, 24, 27, 28, 29, 30, 32, 34, 35, 36, 41, 42, 43, 45, *Ch. 4*, 92, 94, 97, 98, 99, 103, 112, 115, 119

Scot, Reginald, 12, 21, 26, 27
Scotland, 22, 31, 37, 41, 48, 49, 56, 106, 107, 108
Shakespeare, William, 11, 36
Sheldon, Susan, 114
Sowerbutts, Grace, 48
Spain, 36, 63
Spectre, 23, 114, 115, 116, 121
Spee, Friedrich von, 70, 74
Spells, 12, 13, 19, 20, Ch. 4, 70, 87, 89, 92, 94
Spenser, Edmund, 25
Squassation, 73-74, 79, 87, 121
Statutes against witches, 12-15, 63, 67, 68, 87-88, 89, 91, 99, 105
Strappado, 72, 78, 79, 87, 121
Succubi, 13, 121
Swimming of witches, 99-100, 102

Thumbscrews, 78, 79, 87
Tituba, 113, 119
Tompson, Agnes, 37, 41
Torture, 46, 63, 67, 68, 70, 71, 72-73, 74, 78-79, 81, 83, 87, 101, 103, 106, 107
Treves, 75, 78
Trials, 22, 31, 49, 63, 69, 75, 78, 86, 108
 Abingdon (1605), 101
 Bury St. Edmunds (1662), 103, 105
 Chelmsford (1566), 91, 92-93, 94, 97
 Chelmsford (1579), 97
 Chelmsford (St. Osyth witches, 1582), 98
 Chelmsford (1589), 34-35, 98
 Chelmsford (1616), 54
 Chelmsford (1645), 87, 98
 European, Ch. 5
 Kent (1652), 103

Lancashire (1612), 25, 45, 50, 61, 87, 101
North Berwick (1591), 37, 40, 41, 107
Salem, Ch. 7
Salmesbury (1612), 48

Vampires, 11, 12
Veneficia, 15, 22, 98

Walcott, Mary, 114
Waterhouse, Agnes, 91, 92, 94, 97
Waterhouse, Joan, 91, 97
Werewolves, 11, 49, 121
West, William, 19
White magic, 56, 61
Williams, Abigail, 113, 114
Wilson, Bessie, 42, 43
Wilson, Margaret, 41, 42
Witch marks; *see* Devil marks
Witchfinder-general; *see* Matthew Hopkins

Picture Credits

The publishers wish to thank the following for their kind permission to reproduce copyright illustrations on the pages mentioned: Trustees of The British Museum, 17, 20, 23, 46, 52, 65, 68, 71, 72, 73, 82, 95, 96, 106, 111, 116, 117, 118; The Mansell Collection, *Frontispiece*, 10, 13, 18, 22, 29, 30, 33, 34, 38–39, 42, 57, 59, 76–77, 113; The Archbishop of Canterbury and The Trustees of The Lambeth Palace Library, 93; John R. Freeman and Co., 104. Other Illustrations appearing in this book are the property of the Wayland Picture Library.